40 Years in the Gym

Favorite Physical Education Activities

Donald R. Glover, MEd

University of Wisconsin, River Falls

Human Kinetics

Library of Congress Cataloging-in-Publication Data

Glover, Donald R.
  40 years in the gym : favorite physical education activities / Donald R. Glover.
      p. cm.
  ISBN-13: 978-0-7360-6271-8 (soft cover)
  ISBN-10: 0-7360-6271-8 (soft cover)
  1. Physical education for children. I. Title: Forty years in the gym. II. Title.
  GV443.G58 2006
  372.86--dc22

                                      2006006043

ISBN-10: 0-7360-6271-8
ISBN-13: 978-0-7360-6271-8

The Web addresses cited in this text were current as of February 2, 2006, unless otherwise noted.

Acquisitions Editor: Scott Wikgren; **Developmental Editor:** Jacqueline Eaton Blakley; **Assistant Editor:** Bethany J. Bentley; **Copyeditor:** Annette Pierce; **Proofreader:** Jim Burns; **Permission Manager:** Dalene Reeder; **Graphic Designer:** Fred Starbird; **Graphic Artist:** Yvonne Griffith; **Photo Manager:** Sarah Ritz; **Cover Designer:** Keith Blomberg; **Photographer (cover):** Sarah Ritz; **Photographer (interior):** Donald R. Glover. Photo on p. 59 by Lorri Bettenga, **Art Manager:** Kelly Hendren; **Illustrator:** Argosy; **Printer:** United Graphics

Printed in the United States of America   10 9 8 7 6 5 4 3 2 1

Human Kinetics
Web site: www.HumanKinetics.com

United States: Human Kinetics
P.O. Box 5076
Champaign, IL 61825-5076
800-747-4457
e-mail: humank@hkusa.com

Canada: Human Kinetics
475 Devonshire Road Unit 100
Windsor, ON N8Y 2L5
800-465-7301 (in Canada only)
e-mail: orders@hkcanada.com

Europe: Human Kinetics
107 Bradford Road
Stanningley
Leeds LS28 6AT, United Kingdom
+44 (0) 113 255 5665
e-mail: hk@hkeurope.com

Australia: Human Kinetics
57A Price Avenue
Lower Mitcham, South Australia 5062
08 8277 1555
e-mail: liaw@hkaustralia.com

New Zealand: Human Kinetics
Division of Sports Distributors NZ Ltd.
P.O. Box 300 226 Albany
North Shore City
Auckland
0064 9 448 1207
e-mail: info@humankinetics.co.nz

I would like to dedicate this book to physical education, a subject I have been honored to teach for 40 years. I also dedicate it to two physical education teachers, Dan Midura and Mike Wagner. Both are innovative and inspirational teachers who love this subject area and have helped countless other physical educators with their guidance.

Contents

Activity Finder

(continued)

(continued)

Preface

I have been a physical education teacher for 40 years, and I can't think of a better job. Helping students learn movement skills and become healthier has been a very satisfying experience for me. I believe the secret to longevity and joy in my work has been searching for and trying new ideas, then constantly modifying and adapting them for use with my students.

New ideas come from many sources—workshops, books, colleagues, and even students. Over the past 40 years I have created, collected, adapted, and used activities in my classroom from all of these sources and more, and now I would like to share my favorites with you.

The activities in this book are presented in three parts. Part I, Getting Started, includes three chapters' worth of activities that address important teaching themes in the physical education classroom. Chapter 1, Class Organization and Warm-Ups, presents three different methods of organizing and starting your class, along with fun warm-ups suitable for each method. Chapter 2, Character Education, offers innovative and proven ways to use the physical education classroom as a laboratory for teaching important life lessons. Team building is the focus of chapter 3, which contains some of my favorite activities that teach students how to work together to accomplish goals.

Part II, Teaching Movement and Skills, contains activities that will fit nicely into your curriculum because they cover some of the most basic elements taught in physical education. In chapter 4 you will learn some new ways to present rhythms and dances. Chapter 5 follows up the study of rhythms and dance with activities that introduce and practice gymnastics and tumbling. Chapter 6 contains a wealth of activities that teach many common sport skills such as throwing and catching. I think many of us rely on games to indirectly teach skills, but I propose that breaking down skills and using activities and key words to enhance practice of those skills is the most effective way to teach them.

Part III, Putting It All Together, presents activities that combine various elements covered in the first two parts of the book. Chapter 7, Obstacle Courses and Station Activities, offers innovative activities that improve students' motor planning, agility, strength, and endurance. In chapter 8, Interdisciplinary Activities, you will find activities that practice classroom subjects such as math and spelling in a fitness-building context. Some of my favorite competitive games are highlighted in chapter 9. I have written five books about team building and cooperation, but that doesn't mean I don't value competition. If we prepare children to be good teammates and teach them good character, we can help our students to be the best kinds of competitors.

Teaching is both art and science. Deciding when to present fitness activities, rhythms, sport skills, tumbling, character education, team building, and all the other elements of a good program is a science. *How* you present these activities—the way you talk to students, how you interact with them, and how you sell your product—is an art. My hope is that this book helps you with both the art and science of your teaching.

I have tried to go beyond simply presenting activities that cover the major physical education content by sharing with you some unique, proven ways of presenting that content. In my 40 years of teaching, I have found that challenging students with questions such as, "I wonder how many of you think you can do a three-point balance?" is more effective than the traditional method of explaining, demonstrating, and allowing practice. This method not only helps students think through the content and learn it more thoroughly, but also encourages thoughtfulness and creativity. Many of the activities in this book are presented in this questioning style that I used when presenting activities to the students. Even if you find that the questions are not best suited to your teaching situation, you will still have solid, proven activities that your kids will find enjoyable and beneficial.

I hope you enjoy this book. I enjoyed writing it. And I hope these 40 years' worth of ideas and activities give you tangible and lasting benefits throughout your years of teaching.

Acknowledgments

I would like to acknowledge Leigh Anderson, my daughter, for her contributions to the character education discussion in this book. Leigh has brought such innovative ideas to physical education in the past few years. She coauthored *Character Education*, a book every physical educator should have, and continues to be a community builder in all of her endeavors.

Thanks to my St. Mary's University students who helped create many of the team builders in this book. I am continually amazed at your creativity and imagination.

Dan Midura, my teaching partner for the past 10 years, has been a constant source of inspiration and information. I learned many of the games in this book from Dan.

Human Kinetics has provided great leadership in the physical education world. I would like to acknowledge the six developmental editors I have had since 1990 on various books I've written with Human Kinetics, and I would especially like to thank Jackie Blakley for her patience and guidance during the development of this book.

I would also like to acknowledge PE Central for producing www.pecentral.org, the premier Web site for physical educators.

Part I

Getting Started

art I includes three chapters full of activities to help you get your class off to a great start. Chapter 1 leads off the book with warm-up activities grouped by three organizational methods. These are the best of the methods I have tried over the years, and one is exceptional because it makes students feel welcome while firing them up for class. Character education is a hot topic that is gaining popularity in school districts across the United States. In this age of tight school budgets, it makes sense to incorporate this important subject in our physical education classes. Chapter 2 outlines techniques for presenting the concepts of character education in your class and offers some exciting activities that reinforce character education concepts while improving students' fitness.

Team building is another subject area that has grown tremendously over the past decade. Incorporating team building in your physical education class gives your students opportunities to put character education concepts into practice. Chapter 3 features several new team-building challenges to enhance your team-building and character education curriculum.

Chapter *1*

Class Organization and Warm-Ups

As a physical education teacher, I have always been interested in class organization and in discovering the best way to start a physical education class so that the students get excited and look forward to the class activity. When I was a kid in the 1950s, we had no formal warm-up or organization or even a physical education class. The classroom teacher (we had no PE specialists at the time) took us to the gym for a large-group activity. In later years we had recess for a half hour in the morning, which amounted to the teacher saying, "Whoever wants a ball can come and get one," and then out the door we would go. In middle school, we did have a physical education class, which was usually organized by having students count off to form teams or by the teacher assigning students to squads.

I've found that some organizational methods—typically, older ones, such as the squad method—are best only for the instructor (not necessarily the students), because they facilitate assuming roles or forming teams. Traditional warm-ups, such as jumping jacks, push-ups, and other calisthenics, work best in these schemes. As convenient as this method is for teachers, I don't think it does a lot for the enthusiasm of students, who have little or no eye contact or communication with the teacher or other students in these schemes.

In this chapter we explore three newer organizational methods that are better for students, along with warm-up activities that fit each method. The *movement education method* of "find your own space" lends itself to a variety of creative movement warm-ups. The *road method* facilitates movement as soon as the students enter the gym and lends itself to warm-ups that emphasize continuous locomotor movement. The *team method* of organization offers exciting possibilities for community building and character education in your classroom and accommodates a range of possibilities for fun and active warm-up activities.

MOVEMENT EDUCATION METHOD

In the spring of 1967, I attended a workshop called "Movement Education" at Camp Courage in Annandale, Minnesota, that changed the way I thought about organizing and conducting a physical education class. Based on the work of Rudolf Laban, the workshop's main message was that a child develops motor ability in direct proportion to the number of movement patterns he or she experiences. The child creates these patterns while solving movement problems presented by the teacher. Movement education was a new approach not only to organization but also to delivery methods. It involved a movement analysis that people could use to perform sport skills, and it also involved problem solving and a method teachers could use to encourage individuality and creativity among students.

This workshop and Laban's theories were detailed and extensive. However, one of the main principles I took away from the workshop was how to organize a class. "Find a space"—these were the words I used for the next 20 years as the students entered the gym. *"Find a space away from anyone else."* The children quickly ran into the gym and sat in their own spot, and then we started our warm-ups. The warm-ups consisted of Laban's elements of movement in combinations. The combinations of locomotor movements with balance and with relationships to physical education equipment are endless.

Movement Education Warm-Ups

The following movement education activities can be used as warm-ups, or they can be expanded into a 30-minute physical education class. Remember, they all begin with students in their "space" awaiting instructions.

Slow to Fast

GRADES

K–5

EQUIPMENT

- One record player (yes, a record player)
- A 45-rpm or 33-rpm record

DESCRIPTION

One neat thing a record player can do that a CD player can't is change speeds. This is an old warm-up I used when I first started teaching and record players were our source of music.

1. Discuss with the students the different speeds they could use while moving in the gym. They will come up with slow, medium, fast, and faster. Explain to the students that when you play the music, they should move throughout the space to the speed of the music and change the speed of their movement when the speed of the music changes.
2. Put the record on the correct speed and let the students move around the gym using any type of movement they want.
3. Change the speed of the record player. For example, if you have a 45-rpm record, switch it to 33 while it is playing. When this happens the students must change the speed of their movement to match the speed of the music. Challenge them to see how slowly they can move or how quickly and carefully when it switches to 78 rpm.

VARIATION

Have the kids change the way they move every time you switch speeds.

Activity adapted, by permission, from D.R. Glover and L.A. Anderson, 2003, *Character education: 43 fitness activities for community building* (Champaign, IL: Human Kinetics), 88-89.

Dodging

GRADES

K–6

EQUIPMENT

- CD player
- Lively music

DESCRIPTION

1. After the children enter the gym and find their space, ask them "Who can tell me what *dodging* means?" After several responses, settle on the following definition: A quick movement or a quick change of direction or speed or both in order to avoid a collision.

2. Start the music and instruct the children to start jogging anywhere in the gym. Challenge them to see if they can avoid touching anyone else by using their dodging skills.

3. After about one minute of jogging in the full gym, stop the music and challenge them by asking, "Who thinks they can dodge to avoid a collision if we make the space much smaller?" Now move the students to half of the gym, start the music, and let them jog and dodge in the smaller space.

4. After a few minutes in half the gym, move all the students between the end line and the three-point arc, or about one fourth of the gym. Repeat the sequence.

5. Now move the children inside the free throw lane. Jogging and dodging in this small space is exciting and challenging. I always start the students moving very slowly and gradually increase the speed. It is a very difficult task if you ask the students to move quickly.

VARIATIONS

- Use a record player to change speeds.
- Students do the warm-up while holding a ball, which limits the use of the arms.
- To make this much more difficult, add changes in speed, level, or direction or add equipment.

Activity adapted, by permission, from D.R. Glover and L.A. Anderson, 2003, *Character education: 43 fitness activities for community building* (Champaign, IL: Human Kinetics), 86-87.

Pop Goes the Weasel

GRADES

K–5

EQUIPMENT

- A recording of "Pop Goes the Weasel"
- CD or tape player or record player

DESCRIPTION

Let the children move around the gym as the music plays. You may designate a movement or let them move however the music makes them feel. On the first "pop," each child must perform an exercise such as jumping jacks or sit-ups until the next "pop," at which time they must change exercises. Continue this sequence until the song is over.

VARIATIONS

- Let a different student lead the group each time there is a "pop."
- As the children move around the gym, they must change the way they move each time there is a "pop."
- Change balances on "pop" in personal space.
- Pivot and stretch on "pop."

Activity adapted, by permission, from D.R. Glover and L.A. Anderson, 2003, *Character education: 43 fitness activities for community building* (Champaign, IL: Human Kinetics), 88.

||||||||||||| **Locomotor Movements: Direction and Balance** |||||||||||||||||

GRADES //////

K–6

EQUIPMENT //////

- CD player
- Lively music

DESCRIPTION //////

1. Before beginning the activity, ask the students, "How many of you think you can quickly change directions while you are jogging without touching anyone else every time I clap my hands?" Begin the music and have the students start jogging anywhere they want to in the big space. Clap your hands every 10 to 15 seconds to cue students to change directions.

2. After about five or six changes of direction, stop the music. Now ask, "Who thinks they can do a three-point balance and stretch every time I stop the music?" Restart the music. Again, clap your hands about every 15 seconds to signal direction changes, and then encourage and challenge the students to find a different three-point balance when you again stop the music. Continue this sequence for five to six minutes. You may see some of the following balances:

   - Knee, toe, opposite foot, with arms outstretched (see figure 1.1)
   - Two knees and head, with arms outstretched
   - Two feet and one hand, with arms outstretched
   - Two hands and one knee, with leg stretched outward

Figure 1.1   Students create a variety of three-point balances.

VARIATIONS ///////

This warm-up is presented with a lot of variations. Using all of these variations can give you many days of warm-ups.

- Try doing Balance Lesson (see page 73) before this activity.
- Add *levels* to changes in direction. For example, challenge students with the question, "How many can change directions and levels (low, medium, high) every time I clap my hands?"
- Add *speed* (slow, medium, fast) to changes in levels and direction. "Who thinks they can change speed, level, and direction every time I clap?"
- Add or subtract balance points. For example, ask the students to try a *four*-point balance when the music stops.
- Add other movement elements, such as locomotor movements (walk, jump, skip, and so on). Now your challenge may sound like this: "Who thinks they can change locomotor movements as well as direction, level, and speed every time I clap my hands?" or, "Who can find a different way to move every time I signal?" Now the children can add rolling, crawling, animal movements, or any creative movement they can think of.
- Add equipment. For example, ask, "How many can gallop when the music starts and change speeds every time I clap my hands? Who thinks they can do it while dribbling a ball?" Or say, "When the music stops, try adding the ball to your balance." Remind students not to stand on the ball.
- Ask students to work with partners.

||||||||||| Triple Play ||||||||||||||||||||||||||||||||||||||||||||||||||||||||||||||||||||||||||||||||||||||||

GRADES //////

K–5

EQUIPMENT //////

- Lively music
- CD or tape player

DESCRIPTION //////

1. As the students come into the gym and find a space, quickly arrange them into groups of three.
2. Tell the students that when the music starts, they are to hold hands or link arms with their partners and jog around the gym. When the music stops, that is the signal for them to quickly find two new partners and again hold hands or link arms and agree on a new way to move around the gym when the music starts again.
3. Each time the music stops, the students must find a new combination of three and find a new way to move when the music starts.

VARIATIONS //////

- Call out a new way to move each time the students link up.
- Change the type of music after each link-up and tell the students to move to the music. For example, use slow music to encourage sliding, twirling, or walking, and use faster music to encourage running, skipping, or galloping.

|||||||||||| Free Exploration |||||||||||||||||||||||||||||||||||||||||||||||||||||||||||||||||||||

GRADES ||||||

K–3

EQUIPMENT ||||||

- Your choice of equipment (see Description)
- CD player and lively music

DESCRIPTION ||||||

1. After the students enter the gym and find their space, give them the following direction: "Find new ways to use this equipment. The only rule is that you may not bother anyone else. When the music starts, you may begin. When the music stops, please freeze and sit down."

2. Put out hoops, Frisbees, balls, mats, balance beams, hurdles, and so on. When the music starts, the children may practice any skill or movement they want to. This gives the students a chance to show initiative and practice a skill they are interested in.

3. Use this warm-up for at least 10 minutes and watch the children as they work with equipment. You will see a lot of activity. If you want, you may stop the music and ask them to pick another piece of equipment. This warm-up could last the whole period. The only rule I have had is that the students may not bother anyone else, or if they are working with an assigned partner, they may not interrupt other groups.

VARIATIONS ||||||

- Use different pieces of equipment in combination.
- Give students an open-ended question such as, "Can you change the way you are using the equipment?"

|||||||||||| Bridges |||||||||||||||||||||||||||||||||||||||||||||||||||||||||||||||||||||||||||||||

GRADES ||||||

K–5

EQUIPMENT ||||||

Lively music if desired and CD player

DESCRIPTION ||||||

1. After the students come into the gym and find their space, designate half the class as the bridges. The bridges must get on their hands and knees to form a bridge in their space.

2. Tell the rest of the class to start jogging when the music starts. When they come to a bridge they must go under and then over it. (Caution them to be careful when going over a bridge. I made them go *under* first, that way they could not run and try to jump over a bridge, but had to step over or vault over it.)

3. After about two minutes switch the bridges and joggers.

VARIATIONS ||||||

- Let half of the bridges lie flat and the other half make a high bridge (on hands and toes, lifting the seat high in the air), which makes it easy to get under or over (see figure 1.2).
- After joggers go under and over a bridge, they must change the way they move around the gym before going under another bridge.

Figure 1.2   Vary this activity by letting some students lie flat and asking others to make a high bridge.

IIIIIIIIIIIIII **Hustle** IIIIIIIIIIIIIIIIIIIIIIIIIIIIIIIIIIIIIIIIIIIIIIIIIIIIIIIIIIIIIIIIIIIIIIIIIIIIIIIIIIIIIIII

GRADES //////

K–8

EQUIPMENT //////

- One poly spot for every student
- Two beanbags or two tennis balls per student

DESCRIPTION //////

1. As the students enter the gym give each one an indoor base or poly spot and two beanbags. When they have these items they can find their space and sit down. Use as much of the gym as you can so that the students are spread as far from their neighbors as possible. A football or soccer field provides even more space for this warm-up.

2. When the music starts or when the whistle blows, each student runs to a different base, takes a beanbag or ball, and returns with it to his or her own base. Continue until the music stops or, if outside, the whistle sounds.

3. When the music stops players should count the number of beanbags they have on their base. Players are allowed to bring back only one beanbag or ball at a time. A mighty round of applause is given to the players with the highest number of items on their base, and then the music starts or the whistle blows, and the game resumes.

- Do not allow players to take beanbags from their closest neighbor.
- Allow players to bring back two beanbags at a time, but they must be collected from two different bases.
- Players must use a different locomotor movement each time they go after a new beanbag.
- After bringing a beanbag back to their base they must perform five push-ups before going after another beanbag.

ROAD METHOD

Another organizational method I have used is what I call "the road." Quite simply, I built a road around the perimeter of the gym using cones set about 8 to 10 feet (2.4-3 m) in from each corner of the gym. When the children come to the entrance of the gym and hear the music playing, they know they should immediately start jogging slowly on the road. The road is always the same, so children with learning disabilities can quickly learn the route and become accustomed to the routine. Yet the road offers limitless flexibility and variation because it always presents a challenge or a purpose, such as hurdling over small hurdles or weaving through cones. This method maximizes movement time and enhances students' fitness because it requires them to start moving right away.

Warm-Ups on the Road

The following road warm-ups are fun and help develop fitness and coordination. Because features on the road offer a variety of challenges, students are not just mindlessly jogging.

|||||||||||| **Feed Tag** |||||||||||||||||||||||||||||||||||||||||||||||||||||||||||||||||||||||||||||||||

GRADES //////

K–3

EQUIPMENT //////

- Stuffed animal (in this case, Tag the dog)
- Two boxes, each big enough to hold 150 tennis balls, beanbags, or crumpled paper, or a combination of all three
- CD player and lively music

DESCRIPTION //////

As the children come into the gym, the music should be playing. Place Tag at one corner of the road next to his empty food box. At another corner, place the box with Tag's food (see figure 1.3). The children must pick up one piece of food and then jog on the road until they come to Tag's empty box. After they place the food in Tag's box they follow the road to pick up more food to give to Tag. This continues until all the food is gone.

VARIATIONS //////

- Allow the children to bring in their favorite stuffed animal to feed.
- Put out more food if you want the students to have a tougher warm-up.
- Put out less food and allow the children to deliver the food in cars (gym scooters).

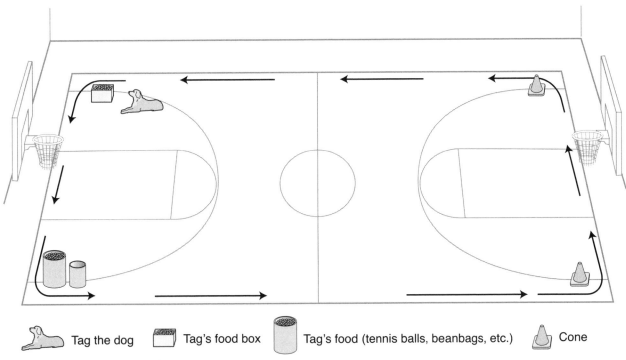

Tag the dog   Tag's food box   Tag's food (tennis balls, beanbags, etc.)   Cone

Figure 1.3   Setup for Feed Tag.

Activity and diagram adapted, by permission, from D.R. Glover and L.A. Anderson, 2003, *Character education: 43 fitness activities for community building* (Champaign, IL: Human Kinetics), 73-74.

Add-On Warm-Up

GRADES

3–8

EQUIPMENT

Music and player (optional)

DESCRIPTION

1. The students report to the gym and start walking the road. As they are walking, organize the students in groups of five. On the signal, students begin jogging around the road together as a team. I prefer to use music as the signal.

2. As the students jog, turn down the music or clap your hands or hit a drum to signal the students to stop and do an exercise led by one of the team members. When finished, the team continues its team jog around the road.

3. Signal again, and another team member leads a new exercise of his or her choice plus five repetitions of the first exercise. When completed, the team continues jogging together.

4. Signal the third time, and another team member leads an exercise of his or her choice plus five repetitions of the second exercise and five repetitions of the first exercise. Continue this sequence until everyone on the team has had a chance to lead an exercise. Whew! This can be a tough warm-up.

VARIATIONS

• Change the way the team moves around the gym after each exercise session.

• Do only one repetition of the previous exercises to make this warm-up easier.

• Do 10 repetitions of each previous exercise.

• Skip the jogging and each team can do the add-on exercise warm-up in its own circle.

IIIIIIIIIIII Snowballs on the Road IIIIIIIIIIIIIIIIIIIIIIIIIIIIIIIIIIIIIIIIIIIIIIIIIIIIIIIIIIIII

GRADES IIIIII

K–6

EQUIPMENT IIIIII

- One piece of construction paper or one page of a newspaper for each student
- Music and player

DESCRIPTION IIIIII

As the students come into the gym, give each student a piece of paper and instruct them to make a tight snowball with it. Once they have done this, start the music, which is their cue to start jogging the road. In this warm-up, however, they must move their snowball around the road with their feet. This continues until all students have completed at least two laps. Now try some of the variations.

VARIATIONS IIIIII

- As the students jog on the road, try to mash their snowballs with your feet, forcing the students to move quickly to avoid a mashing. (Don't really mash their snowballs, just pretend to.)
- Allow several students to act as thieves and try to kick snowballs away from classmates. Ask them, "How many can you kick away before the music stops?"
- Put cones on the road for students to weave in and out of with their snowball.
- Put a goal in each corner of the road for students to hit with their snowball as they jog.

IIIIIIIIIIII Seven Jumps IIIIIIIIIIIIIIIIIIIIIIIIIIIIIIIIIIIIIIIIIIIIIIIIIIIIIIIIIIIIIIIIIIIIIIIIII

GRADES IIIIII

K–5

EQUIPMENT IIIIII

"Seven Jumps" recording and player

DESCRIPTION IIIIII

"Seven Jumps" is a lively folk song and dance that is interrupted by a series of beeps. It has been around for ages. It was old when I started teaching in 1967! This is one of the first warm-ups I ever used.

   As the music plays, the kids move around the road however the music makes them feel. Ask them to do the following when they hear a beep:

- First beep—lie on tummy
- Second beep—lie on back
- Third beep—kneel on knees

When the music starts again, continue moving around the road. The beeps will continue, increasing by one each time. Keep the rotation of tummy, back, and knees throughout the song.

VARIATIONS IIIIII

- Do an exercise such as push-ups or sit-ups during each beep.
- Try a different balance on each beep.

Activity adapted, by permission, from D.R. Glover and L.A. Anderson, 2003, *Character education: 43 fitness activities for community building* (Champaign, IL: Human Kinetics), 87-88.

IIIIIIIIIIII Forest Road IIIIIIIIIIIIIIIIIIIIIIIIIIIIIIIIIIIIIIIIIIIIIIIIIIIIIIIIIIIIIIIIIIIIIIII

GRADES IIIIII

K–6

EQUIPMENT IIIIII

- Three chairs
- Two tables
- Nine cones
- Three 3-inch to 6-inch hurdles
- Music and player (optional)

DESCRIPTION IIIIII

This is my favorite road warm-up and can be used many different ways and in many different versions.

1. Set a cone in each corner of the gym far enough away from the wall to allow students to pass safely between the cone and the wall (see figure 1.4). Students can start walking on the road as soon as they enter the gym (with music playing, if you like).

2. After one or two laps walking, give a signal to change the locomotor movement they are using—skipping, sliding, galloping, jogging, running faster, running with a partner, running with their team, and so on.

3. To make this warm-up even more fun, the next time the students come to the gym, set up obstacles on the road. For example, you could set up hurdles to jump over, tables to go under, cones to weave through, and chairs to go around.

VARIATION

Change the obstacles on the road frequently or add an obstacle each time the students come to class. This will keep the road new and interesting.

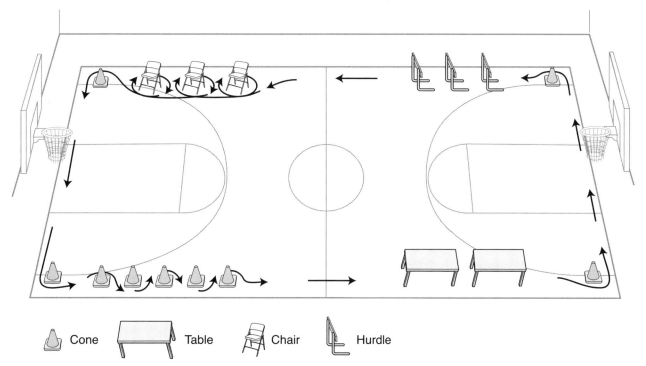

Figure 1.4   Setup for Forest Road.

Activity and diagram adapted, by permission, from D.R. Glover and L.A. Anderson, 2003, *Character education: 43 fitness activities for community building* (Champaign, IL: Human Kinetics), 72-73.

Locomotor Road

GRADES

K–6

EQUIPMENT

- CD player and lively music
- Locomotor cone caps or signs, available from PE equipment retailers such as Gopher Sport (see figure 1.5)

DESCRIPTION

1. Music is playing when the students enter the gym and step on the road. The students can jog slowly for their first lap. Have the cone caps in your hand ready to place them one by one on top of the cones in the corners.

2. Each time the children complete one lap, place a cone cap on one of the corner cones. This directs the students to complete another lap section using a different locomotor skill.

3. You may use only a few of the cone caps or add new cone caps each day to gradually increase the amount of activity.

VARIATIONS

- Complete two laps per cone cap.
- Use fitness station cone caps. Each time students come to a corner of the road, they encounter a different activity posted on the cone. These cone caps are also available from Gopher Sport.
- Use locomotor and fitness station cone caps in combination. For example, put a locomotor skill in each corner with a fitness station in between. Start the kids at different corners.
- Students work out with a partner.

Figure 1.5 Locomotor cone caps from Gopher Sport. The backs are blank so you can write your own instructions in washable marker.

Reprinted by permission of Gopher Sport.

ꜛꜛꜛꜛꜛꜛꜛꜛꜛꜛꜛ Gym Scooter Road ꜛꜛꜛꜛꜛꜛꜛꜛꜛꜛꜛꜛꜛꜛꜛꜛꜛꜛꜛꜛꜛꜛꜛꜛꜛꜛꜛꜛꜛꜛꜛꜛꜛꜛꜛꜛꜛꜛ

GRADES ꜛꜛꜛꜛꜛꜛ

4–6

EQUIPMENT ꜛꜛꜛꜛꜛꜛ

- One gym scooter per two students
- CD player and lively music (optional)

DESCRIPTION ꜛꜛꜛꜛꜛꜛ

Before the students enter the gym, place the scooters upside down along a wall. As soon as the kids enter the gym, divide them into pairs and ask them to jog one lap with their partner. After jogging one lap, one partner turns over a scooter and sits on it, and the partner pushes him or her one lap around the road. At the end of this lap the partners switch jobs. Make sure the kids follow these safety rules:

- Do not race.
- Pushers must keep their hands on their partner at all times.
- Do not collide with other scooters.

VARIATIONS ꜛꜛꜛꜛꜛꜛ

- One partner pushes two laps, then switches.
- The partner on the scooter may take two beanbags and attempt to hit a target or toss the beanbag into a box as he or she is moving.
- Give everyone a scooter and ask them to propel themselves around the road.
- Students must find three different ways to propel their scooter, for example, sitting and pushing with feet, sitting and pulling with feet, and lying and using arms.
- Put out eight fitness station cone caps along the road. As the students propel their scooter along the road they must stop and perform the activity before beginning again.

TEAMS

The *team method* of organizing your physical education class, based on a book titled *Character Education,* which I wrote with my daughter, Leigh Ann Anderson (2003, Human Kinetics), offers exciting ways to enhance community and character building in your classrooms and to help you achieve National Association for Sport and Physical Education (NASPE) standards 5 and 6.

- **Standard 5:** Exhibits responsible personal and social behavior that respects self and others in physical activity settings.
- **Standard 6:** Values physical activity for health, enjoyment, challenge, self-expression, and/or social interaction.

I now use the team method to start and organize my class about 90 percent of the time, with movement education and the road providing something different for the remaining class meetings.

Team discussion on pages 15-18 adapted, by permission, from D.R. Glover and L.A. Anderson, 2003, *Character education: 43 fitness activities for community building* (Champaign, IL: Human Kinetics), 23-32.

Allowing students to work in teams is a great way to build community in the physical education classroom. Placing students in a smaller-group setting helps establish a safe, friendly atmosphere. Beginning class with a group of people with whom students feel comfortable and accepted is the first step in creating an ideal learning environment. The more students know and trust those around them, the more willing they will be to open themselves up and take risks.

Ideally, each team should have six to eight students, with each student assigned a number within the team. For example, each team has a one, two, three, and so on. This gives you a lot of flexibility to mix up teams for activities, for example, "All twos get together on one team" or "All even numbers on one team, and all odd numbers on the other team." At the beginning of the year, have teams create their own name, handshake, and cheer. If the teacher has examples of sports teams doing fancy handshakes or cheers, they should show the students to give them an idea of what they are. Invite athletes from the high school to model what their team does as a special cheer or handshake. Once you have decided the makeup of the teams, the students should always report directly to their team when class begins.

I keep my teams intact all year long. You could change them periodically if you wish. The advantage of changing the team makeup is that the students will form new relationships. Keeping the teams together all year allows students to build strong bonds and function well together.

Using Motivators

A *motivator* is an enthusiastic verbal and physical action that recognizes each student entering the gym or joining his or her team. The purpose is to make students feel welcomed and get them fired up for class. Another reason for the motivator is to teach students how to acknowledge people in a friendly way and why this is important. So often as a teacher, I have seen students in the hallway who won't say hello unless I say it first. Moreover, I rarely have seen students who are already sitting in class acknowledge their classmates as they enter. They look up at the person, make eye contact, and then look away. This sets an unfriendly tone, and it also makes it possible for some students to go through a whole day without being acknowledged. We need to make students aware of how greeting people can make them feel. Ask them how they would feel if they entered a room and everyone looked up at them and then looked away. Then give them the other scenario of someone acknowledging them in a friendly way. Help them realize how they might make people feel with their actions. Are they the students who look away or are they the ones who smile, make eye contact, and say hello?

The motivator should be done each class period in order to establish a sense of belonging and a feeling of significance to make sure that each child feels as though it truly matters that he or she came. This feeling must be established immediately to make students feel more comfortable and help eliminate any fears they might have walking into class. Motivators can be accomplished in a variety of ways including the teacher standing at the door as students enter, high-fiving them while saying their name. However, as easy as it may sound, this may be difficult for teachers who have back-to-back classes and lack the time to set up and take down before and after each class. Following are several ways to ensure that each student is enthusiastically recognized when entering class.

• **Teacher Leads.** The teacher stands at the door and high-fives students as they walk in. It's important that the teacher portray an *enthusiastic* attitude while saying hello *and saying each student's name.* Enthusiasm is important because you want to motivate the students for class as well as let them know you are excited they are there.

• **Student Leads.** A student stands at the door and greets students in the same manner as in the teacher-led motivator. It is important that the student volunteer do this rather than a teacher appoint someone who is unwilling. It's also important to discuss the attitude of the motivator before students take on this role. You may want to model enthusiastic greetings with the students and have them practice these greetings with each other. As a class, students could also brainstorm different words to use as greetings so that the motivator has lots of options, for example, *Hello, Jim! Good to see you, Kathy! Welcome to class, Mark!* The student's responsibility is to greet each student by saying his or her name after the words he or she chooses as a greeting. The student motivator is an important role in making people feel welcomed and motivating them. Students should practice this role on each other before you allow them to perform it. Don't allow students to be enthusiastic when they greet some students and not when they greet others. This defeats the purpose of the greeting and has the potential to hurt feelings. Address these issues and revisit them throughout the year.

• **Teams.** Each team uses the team handshake they came up with at the beginning of the year. Each student is responsible for shaking every team member's hand while greeting them and saying their name.

• **Follow the Leader.** Give each team a chance to model its handshake, then direct the rest of the class to use it to greet three other people. For example, say, "Today we are going to greet each other using team A's handshake. Team A, show us your handshake and greet your teammates in your most enthusiastic way, making sure to say the name of the student you greet." Team A models its handshake as the rest of the class watches. Then say, "Now greet at least three other people using team A's handshake." If there are five teams, the class has five different handshakes to use as motivators.

• **Birds of a Feather.** Each person on a team should have a number, so you can ask all the ones greet each other, all the twos, and so on. The greeting could be a simple high-five or, to involve the students, let a student who has a birthday that month or a student who is great at encouraging others pick the handshake that the class will use.

• **One Team Stands at the Door Greeting Students.** This is a fun motivator that works more like a cheer. It is similar to introducing starters before a basketball game, where teammates line up and players run out to center court, high-fiving their teammates as their name is announced. In this particular motivator a team stands in a line at the door greeting the rest of the class with high fives as they run in. Instead of saying, "Hello, Jim" or "Welcome, Mark," they say things like, "Way to go, Jim!" "You're awesome, Mark!" "All right, Tina!" Again, students could brainstorm possible ways to cheer on their teammates. Allow students to get loud and crazy because you want them to be fired up. Some students are more comfortable motivating others when they are with their teammates rather than by themselves. Expect teams to be a bit quiet the first time they perform this motivator. Don't worry, the more they get to know and trust those around them, the more enthusiastic they will become.

• **Double Team.** This motivator can get loud and crazy, but it is fun for those who won't have the opportunity to be on a team outside of physical education class. This motivator is similar to the previous one, except that two teams stand at the door, one on each side. As students enter, they high-five classmates on both sides of them. Again, encourage the teams doing this motivator to get into it and cheer on their teammates enthusiastically as they enter the gym.

Being enthusiastic is an important factor in motivating students. This may be easy for the teacher, but how can we get students to portray enthusiastic attitudes? First of all, it has to come from the students themselves; a teacher can't make students be enthusiastic. The teacher must model it as much as possible and hope the students learn from example. Second, it's more likely that enthusiastic attitudes will surface if students are excited about the class. The teacher must make physical education a place where all students *want* to be.

There are always students who are more enthusiastic than the rest. Most likely, these students will volunteer to be the motivators at the door early in the year. If some students never volunteer to be at the door, that is fine. Never make a student take on a role he or she is not comfortable with. Some of the more reserved students may be more enticed to take on the motivator role if they have the option to stand and greet with a partner.

A set schedule for motivators in which students come to class and perform the motivators on their own without teacher direction is an ideal setup. For example, if a team stands at the door to motivate every Wednesday, and the teams are on a rotating schedule, then teams should know ahead of time when their turn will be. This is an optimal situation, but it might take a while for your classes to get there.

Once the students get used to a schedule, the teacher should begin to reduce the amount of directions he or she gives students to get them going. The directions should turn into questions, for example, "What team is leading the handshake today? Could you please show us what to do? What do you need to remember when greeting a classmate?" If the teacher doesn't have a set schedule, he or she could assign the motivator during the previous class period. For example, she could say, "Who hasn't had a chance to be the motivator at the door and would like to be?" In this case the student or students who volunteer will know they can either stand at the door motivating students as they walk in, or they could simply have a handshake ready to model and say, "Motivate everyone on your team with this handshake and remember to say their name while greeting them."

Team Warm-Ups

Team warm-ups are different from movement education or on-the-road warm-ups because they are done in teams rather than individually. This puts the focus on team spirit and community. Emotional and social connections can be strengthened when teams work out or warm up together.

‖‖‖‖‖‖ **Team Link** ‖‖

GRADES ‖‖‖‖

K–6

EQUIPMENT ‖‖‖‖

Lively music and player

DESCRIPTION ‖‖‖‖

I like this warm-up because it is like a moving team builder. The students must work together and constantly communicate about speed and direction in order to remain linked. Not only do teammates have to communicate with each other, but the groups also have to communicate with each other in order to avoid collisions.

1. After teams link, challenge them by asking, "Which team thinks they can stay linked even though we will change locomotor movements five times?" Remind teams to be careful not to collide with other linked teams. Teams should link in one of the following ways:

Holding hands in a straight line

Holding hands in a circle

Linking arms in a straight line, side by side

Linking arms in a circle

Placing hands on shoulders in a straight line, one behind the other

Placing hands on hips in a straight line, one behind the other

Placing hands on shoulders in a straight line, side by side

Combinations of any of these

2. When the music starts or when you say go, groups must run anywhere they want to in the gym, but they must not break their links.

3. When you give a signal (whistle, hand clap, stop the music, or the like), the students must change the way they move, skipping, galloping, and so on, without breaking their links.

VARIATIONS ||||||

- On the change signal, students must link to someone new before changing the way they move.

- On the change signal, students must link next to someone new and also change how they are linked before changing the way they move.

|||||||||||| Exercise Card Warm-Up ||||||||||||||||||||||||||||||||||||||||||||||||||||||||||||||||

GRADES ||||||

K–6

EQUIPMENT ||||||

- Note cards with an exercise or activity listed on each one
- Lively music and player

DESCRIPTION ||||||

1. Make exercise cards by writing on an index card the name of an exercise and the number of repetitions you would like your students to do. You can laminate the cards and include a drawing of a stick figure performing the exercise. Exercises might be knee push-ups, 10 repetitions; kangaroo jumps, 10 repetitions; or sit-ups, 10 repetitions. Each student gets an exercise card.

2. Tell the students what method they should use to move around the gym. When the music starts, the students move wherever they want, and they do not have to move together as a team.

3. When the music stops, students must find a team member. They give each other a high five while yelling the name of their team. Next, they exchange cards and perform the exercises on them.

4. This continues until each team member has been greeted by every other person on their team. If there is an uneven number of students on a team, three students can greet each other and exchange cards.

VARIATIONS ||||||

- Use Gopher Sport's physical education activity cards (www.gophersport.com/products. cfm?cl=1790&pid=1042) for some wild options, for example: Each team member has a PE activity card, and the team members move together in the gym while the music plays. When the music stops, students must do one of the activities before the music starts again. For example, everyone in the group must join hands to form a triangle, or everyone in a team must line up in birthday order starting with January.

- Give one team an activity card for each member. When the music starts, the team with the cards are "it" and can tag anyone in the gym. When they do, the person tagged must perform the activity on the card. Next round, let another team be the taggers.

Builders and Wreckers

GRADES

K–6

EQUIPMENT

- As many pins and cones as you can find
- Music and player (optional)

DESCRIPTION

1. Assign two teams to be the builders and two teams to be the wreckers. Scatter the cones and pins throughout the gym.
2. On the go signal or when the music starts, the wreckers use their hands to tip over the cones, and the builders reset them. Both groups move as quickly as they can. At the end of two minutes or when the music stops, count how many cones are standing.
3. Now switch jobs and see if the new builders can stand up more cones than the previous builders could.

VARIATIONS

- Change locomotor movements.
- Change the method used to knock over cones, for example, knock them down with the elbow, knee, or shoulder.

Circuits

GRADES

2–8

EQUIPMENT

- Circuit card
- Six to eight jump ropes
- Two mats
- Two cones
- Six to eight gym scooters
- Popular music and player (optional)

DESCRIPTION

1. Teammates report to their team huddle.
2. Assign a captain for each team. Call each captain forward and give them their team's circuit warm-up sheet. Each team's sheet lists the same circuit exercises but in a different order for each team. This prevents two teams from being at the same station at once.
3. Teams must complete all activities on the sheet together as a team. Team members may not run ahead and finish early.

Consider playing popular music during this warm-up and using it as a signal: "Once the music starts you may begin and when the music stops, please freeze and sit down in a circle with your team." A sample circuit could look like the following (see figure 1.6):

- Touch eight separate lines on the floor with your right hand.
- Complete 50 jump rope repetitions.
- Jog five laps around the perimeter of the gym.
- Report to the push-up mat and attempt 20 push-ups. You may use your knees.
- Touch four separate walls with your left hand.
- Report to the sit-up mat. Attempt 20 sit-ups.
- Slide step or shuffle step eight widths of the gym.
- Report to the gym scooters. Lie on your tummy on the scooter. Complete six trips around the cones, using your arms to propel the scooter.
- Sing a song with two verses to your teacher.
- Report to the cage ball. Roll the cage ball around the circle 10 times. Teammates should form a circle with their backs to the inside of the circle. Ball will roll around the outside of the circle.

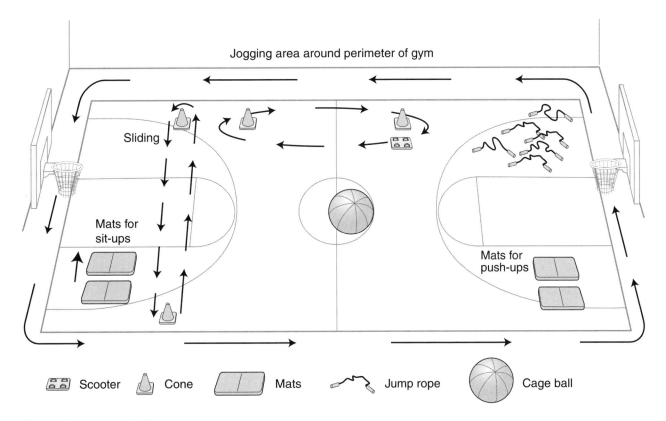

Figure 1.6 Setup for Circuits.

Activity and diagram adapted, by permission, from D.R. Glover and L.A. Anderson, 2003, *Character education: 43 fitness activities for community building* (Champaign, IL: Human Kinetics), 68-70.

|||||||||||| Save Easter |||||||||||||||||||||||||||||||||||||||||||||||||||||||||||||||||||||||||||||||||||||||||||

GRADES //////

K–3

EQUIPMENT //////

- At least five "bunnies" (small items such as beanbags, tennis balls, crumpled paper, shuttle-cocks) per student
- One bucket or box per team

DESCRIPTION //////

This is a great warm-up for younger children that can be done outdoors or in the gym. Place all the "bunnies" in the field before class begins (see figure 1.7). Each child should have at least five chances to save a bunny, so you need a lot of bunnies—for a class of 30 students, for example, you need about 150.

1. Each team gathers around its bucket or box. Tell students that on your signal, they must run out into the field and bring back one baby bunny and put it in the bucket before a storm comes and the baby bunnies can't find their way home.

2. On your signal, all team members run out into the field and gather up a baby bunny. They then run back and place it in their bucket or box. The team members continue until all baby bunnies are collected.

3. Students can bring back only one baby bunny at a time. The farther the bunnies are away from the buckets, the greater the workout for the students.

4. After all the bunnies have been saved and they are resting in their bucket or box, the students can take two or three and run out into the field and scatter the bunnies for the next class.

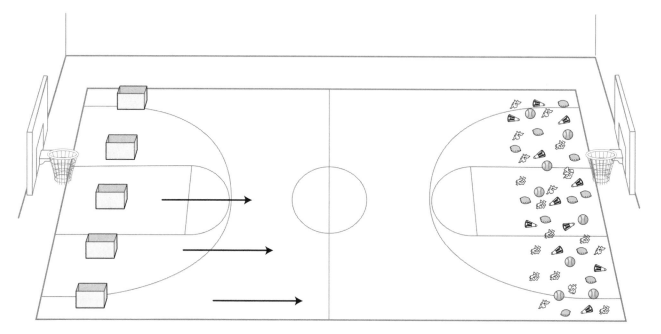

Figure 1.7   Setup for Save Easter.

Activity and diagram adapted, by permission, from D.R. Glover and L.A. Anderson, 2003, *Character education: 43 fitness activities for community building* (Champaign, IL: Human Kinetics), 74-75.

ⅠⅠⅠⅠⅠⅠⅠⅠⅠⅠⅠ **Sports Mobile** ⅠⅠⅠ

GRADES ⅠⅠⅠⅠⅠ

1–6

EQUIPMENT ⅠⅠⅠⅠⅠ

Sports music "Jock Jams" or other lively music and player

DESCRIPTION ⅠⅠⅠⅠⅠ

1. Assign each team a sport. For example, for four teams of six, the sports could be basketball, football, softball, and volleyball. Each team identifies six skills related to that sport. (You may have to demonstrate these skills to the younger children.) For basketball, the skills could be jump-shooting, rebounding, dribbling, passing, defensive sliding, and shooting free throws. For football the skills could be hiking, blocking, punting, passing, receiving, and carrying the ball through tacklers. For softball the skills could be batting, pitching, throwing from center field, stretching to make a catch on first base, fielding a ground ball at shortstop and throwing to first, and bunting. For volleyball the skills could be bumping, overhead passing, serving, spike-blocking, digging, and rolling.

2. Assign each child a skill for his or her team's sport. When the music starts, each student acts out his or her skill. When music momentarily stops, each team member chooses a new skill to act out when the music starts again. Continue until every team member has acted out all of his or her assigned sport skills. Encourage the teams to get into it and pretend that they are playing in a championship game, performing the skills as intensely as possible.

VARIATIONS ⅠⅠⅠⅠⅠ

- Conduct a long warm-up with each team taking a turn with each sport.
- Use an overhead projector so the teams' shadows show on the wall. The students can make their shadows perform the skill.
- Line up the team in a straight line, with members performing their skill one at a time. Keep repeating and work toward a smoothly running mobile.
- Videotape and play back the sports mobile movements. The students will enjoy seeing their mobile function.

Activity adapted, by permission, from D.R. Glover and L.A. Anderson, 2003, *Character education: 43 fitness activities for community building* (Champaign, IL: Human Kinetics), 95-96.

ⅠⅠⅠⅠⅠⅠⅠⅠⅠⅠⅠ **Pick a Card** ⅠⅠ

GRADES ⅠⅠⅠⅠⅠ

1–8

EQUIPMENT ⅠⅠⅠⅠⅠ

- Exercise cards
- Music and player (optional)

DESCRIPTION ⅠⅠⅠⅠⅠ

Teams can do this warm-up on the road, or they can go wherever they want in the gym.

1. As students report to their team huddle, give each captain a card with a locomotor skill printed on it. (You can make these by writing locomotor movements on cards. These could

include skip, hop, jump, gallop, slide, twirl, leap, tiptoe, march, and run or combinations such as run-gallop-jump.)

2. On your signal, the team performs its locomotor skill, moving as a team wherever they please throughout the gym.

3. Signal again, and the captains for that day exchange cards and the team performs the new locomotor movement.

4. Continue until all teams have performed all locomotor movements.

VARIATIONS ///////

- Give a new card to the captains on every signal; this allows the team to perform many more locomotor movements.
- Add music.
- Add an exercise, such as push-ups, to the locomotor skill on the card.
- Add equipment. For example, the card might say, "Skip until the teacher's whistle, then get a volleyball and serve 20 times to a partner."

Activity adapted, by permission, from D.R. Glover and L.A. Anderson, 2003, *Character education: 43 fitness activities for community building* (Champaign, IL: Human Kinetics), 82-83.

|||||||||||| Leader of the Pack ||||||||||||||||||||||||||||||||||||||||||||||||||||||||||||||||||||||||||||

GRADES //////

1–8

EQUIPMENT //////

None needed unless variations are used

DESCRIPTION //////

1. After students report to their team, you or the team captain assigns one locomotor movement to each team member. These could include walk, jog, run, skip, gallop, and jump. Other movements could include gallop with other foot leading, hop, leap, slide, and walk backward.

2. On the signal, teammate one leads his or her team around the gym doing the assigned locomotor movement.

3. After 30 to 50 seconds, blow a whistle, bang a drum, or yell "change." On this signal, the leader goes to the back of the line. Teammate two is now in front, and the team will follow the new leader and do the new locomotor movement. Each leader is free to move anywhere in the gym with the team following behind. Each teammate gets a chance to lead.

VARIATIONS //////

- Add music.
- Add equipment. For example, if you add a basketball, try the following:
    - Teammate one leads 30 seconds of jogging and 60 seconds of chest passing.
    - Teammate two leads 30 seconds of jumping and 60 seconds of bounce passing.
    - Teammate three leads 30 seconds of skipping and 60 seconds of dribbling.
    - Teammate four leads 30 seconds of galloping and 60 seconds of shooting layups.
    - Teammate five leads 30 seconds of running and 60 seconds of pivoting and stretching.
    - Teammate six leads 30 seconds of walking and 60 seconds of ball-handling drills.

Activity adapted, by permission, from D.R. Glover and L.A. Anderson, 2003, *Character education: 43 fitness activities for community building* (Champaign, IL: Human Kinetics), 83-84.

Hungry Snakes

GRADES

K–5

EQUIPMENT

- One ball bag or garbage bag for each team
- Paper balls, beanbags, tennis balls, or any other objects to use as "food"
- Music and player

DESCRIPTION

1. Scatter objects (food) evenly across the gym. Members of each group line up one behind the other. The first student in the line is the head of the snake. The last student is the stomach of the snake and holds the bag or garbage can. The rest of the students form the body of the snake.

2. All members of the snake must stay connected by holding hands, linking arms, holding the shoulders of the person in front of them, or using any other method they can come up with. If the snake becomes disconnected, they must dump the food out of their stomach.

3. The snakes are very hungry and must travel around the gym to collect food. The head of the snake picks up food and passes the object through every person in line all the way to the stomach. The last person then puts the food in the stomach.

4. Start the music to signal to the students that they can begin moving. After a snake collects three food objects, the head goes to the back to become the stomach, and the person now in the front becomes the head.

5. The new head must change the level, speed, or motion of the movement. As a class, see how many food items the snakes can collect. Once this warm-up is finished, have students sit in their snake groups to count their food.

Team Frozen Tag

GRADES

K–6

EQUIPMENT

Music and player (optional)

DESCRIPTION

The following tag games are fast paced and competitive, so you might want to have the kids stretch or jog a lap before playing.

1. Three students are designated as "it"; the rest scatter in the gym.

2. When you give a signal, such as music or a whistle, the taggers try to tag as many classmates as they can. Primary students should hold a foam ball or Frisbee to help tag. Remind them that a tag is not a push. Classmates try to avoid a tag by fleeing.

3. When a tagged person is frozen, he or she must raise one hand and can be unfrozen only if a member of their team gives him or her a high five.

4. Change taggers every two minutes.

VARIATIONS

- To unfreeze someone, a team member must slide on the floor between frozen teammates' legs.
- Use more or fewer taggers.

|||||||||||| **Tail Tag** |||||||||||||||||||||||||||||||||||||||||||||||||||||||||||||||||||||||||||||||||||||||||||||||||||||||||||||||||||

GRADES ||||||

K–6

EQUIPMENT ||||||

Lively music and player (optional)

DESCRIPTION ||||||

1. After the students are greeted and report to their teams, they should do a team break. Doing a team break involves everyone putting their hands in the middle as they yell their own name.

2. Instruct the students to line up one behind the other in a straight line, with both hands on the waist of the person in front of them. The first person in line steps forward and turns to face the rest of the team.

3. When the music starts, the person in front of the connected team attempts to tag the last person in line (the tail). The people in the middle and the last person must move quickly in order to keep the first person from tagging the tail.

4. If the first person tags the tail, then the tagger becomes the new tail and the person now in front becomes the new tagger. Stop the music every 60 seconds or so and allow the children to rotate. This gives everyone a chance to be a tagger.

VARIATION ||||||

Keep everyone connected and facing forward. Now the front person has to try to catch the last person while still connected to the team.

|||||||||||| **Team Toss Tag** |||||||||||||||||||||||||||||||||||||||||||||||||||||||||||||||||||||||||||||||||||||||||||||

GRADES ||||||

1–12

EQUIPMENT ||||||

- Two 5-inch or 6-inch (13-15 cm) foam balls
- Six colored vests or pinnies

DESCRIPTION ||||||

This tagging game has it all: passing, catching, teamwork, strategy, dodging, and running. Divide the gym or a large playing area into as many sections as there are taggers (see figure 1.8 for setup). For this description, we use a team of six as our taggers.

1. Divide the gym into six sections and place a tagger in each section. Put a colored vest or pinnie on each tagger. The taggers cannot leave their sections. The rest of the students can move freely anywhere they want to in order to avoid a tag. The taggers can only tag people in their section and they can only tag with a foam ball.

2. To start the game, give two taggers a foam ball. As the students flee the sections to avoid a tag, the taggers must pass the ball to their teammate tagger in the other sections in order to tag a student.

3. Once tagged, the student must freeze, and in order to reenter the game, he or she must receive a high five from another student on their team.

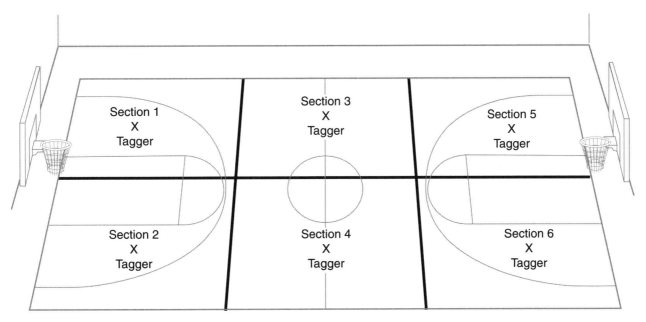

Figure 1.8   Setup for Team Toss Tag.

VARIATIONS ||||||

- Add or subtract tagger sections.
- Add more balls.
- Use bigger balls and a smaller area for very young kids.
- Divide up a football field and use footballs.

Activity and diagram adapted, by permission, from D.R. Glover and L.A. Anderson, 2003, *Character education: 43 fitness activities for community building* (Champaign, IL: Human Kinetics), 93-94.

|||||||||||| **Locomotor Tag** ||||||||||||||||||||||||||||||||||||||||||||||||||||||||||||||||||||||||||||||||||||||||||||||||

GRADES ||||||

K–6

EQUIPMENT ||||||

- Colored pinnies
- Exercise cards

DESCRIPTION ||||||

1. Give two, three, or four students a pinnie with an exercise card pinned or taped to it. When the music starts, the students with the exercise pinnies attempt to tag as many classmates as possible.
2. When tagged, the student must perform the exercise that is taped to the tagger's pinnie. After performing the exercise, he or she can rejoin the game.
3. After three or four minutes, allow four more students to be taggers or change the exercises on the pinnies.

Rip-Flag Scramble

GRADES

K–12

EQUIPMENT

- One rip-flag belt and rip flag per student
- Five or six poly spot bases

DESCRIPTION

Although students will report to their teams before these next two warm-ups; the games do not necessarily have to be played as teams. Dan Midura, teaching partner and coauthor of *Team Building Through Physical Challenges,* gave them to me. Rip-Flag Scramble is a simple, yet very effective, running game that allows for a great deal of participation. A basketball court–sized area provides plenty of space for up to 35 students. This activity can be done indoors as well as outdoors. (See figure 1.9 for setup.)

1. To prepare for the game, randomly place five or six bases throughout the play area. Give each student one rip-flag belt and one rip flag. To choose chasers, take the flags from about six students. Use an organizational technique to choose the chasers such as "Everyone with an August birthday, please give me your flag."

2. Explain that a student will be a chaser only until he or she rips off someone's flag. When a chaser successfully grasps a flag, the chaser puts that flag on his or her own belt and becomes a runner. The person losing the flag temporarily becomes the new chaser. A person is only a chaser when he or she does not have a flag. If a flag falls onto the floor, anyone without a flag may pick it up and put it onto his or her belt.

3. The bases are to be used as safe or free places. A student standing on a base is safe from the chasers. However, if another student comes to an occupied base, the student on the base must leave. The last student to come to a base becomes the temporary owner of that base. A student must go to a different base before returning to any base on which he or she has previously stood.

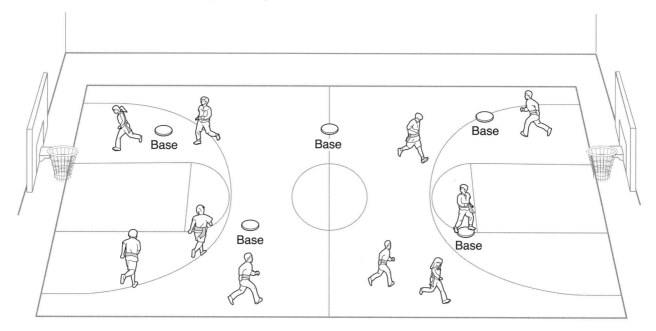

Figure 1.9 Setup for Rip-Flag Scramble.

4. One of the most important elements of this game is the "polite rules." Students arriving at an occupied base must speak politely to the student on that base. Use phrases such as the following: "Pardon me." "Excuse me, please." "Thank you for your base." "Happy day, see you soon." Students may not push someone off a base and say, "Get out of here."

5. By using the polite rules, an attitude of friendly play develops rather than a feeling of competing against one another.

Activity and diagram adapted, by permission, from D.W. Midura and D.R. Glover, 1999, *The competition-cooperation link: Games for developing respectful competitors* (Champaign, IL: Human Kinetics), 47-49.

||||||||||||| Fastest Tag in the World |||||||||||||||||||||||||||||||||||||||||||||||||||||||

GRADES //////

K–12

EQUIPMENT //////

No equipment is needed unless you need cones for marking boundary lines.

DESCRIPTION //////

1. Students begin by standing in their personal space. Be certain that no one can touch another person or a wall. All students are chasers, and every student can tag every other student.

2. When you clap your hands, all students attempt to run from each other while trying to tag other people. Once a person is tagged, he or she is temporarily frozen. While frozen, a student may not move his or her feet and legs or bend at the hips. A frozen student may however, reach out and tag anyone running. If two students tag one another at the same time, they are both frozen.

3. After about 15 seconds, in which time most of the students have been frozen, clap your hands and say, "Fastest tag in the world; you're free" (or give a signal of your choice). Everyone is unfrozen and is free to run and tag again. You will probably clap your hands and allow freedom to the students 6 to 10 times before calling for a break.

4. This game is intended to be a quick warm-up or introductory activity in class. Play it for only a few minutes. There is no need to declare winners in this game.

Activity adapted, by permission, from D.W. Midura and D.R. Glover, 1999, *The competition-cooperation link: Games for developing respectful competitors* (Champaign, IL: Human Kinetics), 51-53.

Chapter **2**

Character Education

We want our students to graduate from high school with something more in their minds than just the facts, figures, and skills that teachers present. We would also like our students to exhibit certain behaviors and attitudes, such as respect and honesty. These qualities won't just appear spontaneously; parents and teachers must nurture them.

It is important to teach *character education* using the best teaching method we have—by example. Teachers, principals, cooks, custodians, teacher's aides, secretaries, bus drivers, and all who come in contact with students during the day are potential role models. All of these people should be committed to ethical behavior and to the character education ideals of the school.

Character education should include formal as well as informal instruction, and physical education offers a rich laboratory that can provide insight into how good character works. Opportunities for building character in PE classes include accepting judgment calls, trusting your teammates, and keeping your poise, just to name a few.

In this chapter, we explore ways to integrate character education into your physical education classroom—through discussion of focus words, reflection on character education scenarios, and participation in fitness activities that emphasize character building.

FOCUS WORDS

We should take time to teach and highlight the values we want our students to exhibit in physical education. I suggest concentrating the discussion on a list of 19 *focus words* outlined in this section. You should explain, discuss, and visually highlight these words in the gym.

Of course physical education is an activity class, so long discussions cannot happen every class period, but try to introduce and discuss one word every two weeks and see how it helps to promote ethical behavior. If you don't feel you can take the time for discussion in your class, then perhaps introduce the word and meaning and send home the discussion questions for the parents to administer. Another option is to work with classroom teachers to carry the topic over into their classroom discussions. We're always looking for ways to connect disciplines, and this is a great opportunity. Bringing a high school athlete into your classroom to lead the discussion adds volume to its importance.

You can reinforce the teaching of these focus words in many creative ways. Have students make posters containing these words and their meanings and fill the gym walls with them. Mark playground balls with the words. Print words such as sportsmanship, tolerance, and pride on the balls the kids use for foursquare, kickball, and so on. Other types of equipment you could mark with character education words include cones, bats, and beanbags. Be creative. Find ways to keep these words in focus the entire year.

Dicussion of focus words on pp. 31-37 adapted, by permission, from D.R. Glover and L.A. Anderson, 2003, *Character education: 43 fitness activities for community building* (Champaign, IL: Human Kinetics), 41-50.

Respect

Definition: A feeling of honor or esteem for something or someone

Teaching point: During competition, show respect for your opponents, your teammates, and the officials. If you understand that everyone is doing their best, then show respect for their efforts.

Discussion questions:

- Do you want people to respect you?
- What are some ways you can earn respect?
- What makes you respect others?
- Have you ever seen anyone show disrespect for their teammates? For their opponents? For the officials?
- What did you think of that behavior?
- Can you respect property as well as a person?

Honesty

Definition: Truthfulness and trustworthiness and not lying, stealing, or cheating

Teaching point: George Washington, our first president, said that the best attribute a person can possess is that they are known for their honesty.

Discussion questions:

- Can you think of anyone you know who is completely honest?
- Can someone be dishonest during a game? How?
- What would happen if teams of dishonest players competed against one another?
- Is taking performance-enhancing drugs dishonest? How?

Sportsmanship

Definition: Observing the rules of a contest and accepting victory or defeat without behaving boastfully or angrily

Teaching point: We should all play hard, but we should play fairly and be honest with our teammates and opponents. Try to be the best you can be, but be considerate of others and fair in your treatment of others.

Discussion questions:

- Have you ever been a poor sport? What happened that caused you to become a poor sport at that time?
- Can parents be poor sports? How?
- Can coaches be poor sports? How?
- How can someone show good sportsmanship?
- Why do you think good sportsmanship is important?

Trust

Definition: To place confidence or firm belief in the honesty or dependability of someone or something

Teaching point: You have to trust in your future, and if you prepare and work hard, your dreams have a better chance of coming true.

Discussion questions:
- Do you trust some people more than you trust others? Why?
- What makes people trustworthy?
- Is it important for your parents to trust you?
- How can you show trust in your coach or teacher?

Judgment

Definition: The ability to reach decisions after careful consideration of evidence, the ability to choose wisely

Teaching point: You are the best judge of what you can do and what you cannot; be honest with yourself and do what is right.

Discussion questions:
- What are some of the judgments you need to make during the school day?
- Do some judgments include thinking about the effect that your decisions have on other people?

Make up a situation. Use good judgment and act out the situation. Try it again only this time use bad judgment. For example, during physical education class, your team is playing basketball against your best friend's team. Your team loses a close game, and your friend taunts you. He or she is only kidding but you get very angry. What happens?

Good judgment: Bad judgment:

Pride

Definition: A sense of one's own dignity or worth

Teaching point: Always do your best in school and in life. Give your best effort; if you do not, you cheat yourself and others. Take pride in yourself.

Discussion questions:
- How do you cheat yourself if you do not do your best?
- How can athletes take pride in their sport?
- How can students take pride in their schoolwork?
- Can you take pride in your behavior and treatment of others?
- How many of you have pride in your school? Why or why not?

Integrity

Definition: Strict personal honesty and independence

Teaching point: You must believe in your own honesty and character before you can believe in anyone else's. People will believe in you if you have integrity.

Discussion questions:
- Integrity has another meaning. It can also mean unity or completeness. So what would the statement, "The integrity of the team has been kept," mean to you?
- I think the meaning of this focus word is that you can be honest and fair even if no one else is behaving that way. That sounds difficult; do you think you could do it?

Character

Definition: A person's normal nature or behavior

Teaching point: Build your house on a strong foundation of brick and mortar so that it stands for 100 years. Build your character on a foundation of honesty, respect, and discipline so that your reputation stands for 100 years.

Discussion questions:

- Does your character include many different behaviors, such as honesty, good sportsmanship, respect, and so on?
- What is the difference between having character and being a character?
- What do you think is the best aspect of your character?

Poise

Definition: Dignity and possession, or control, of your behavior; composure

Teaching point: How you respond to different things that happen to you shows if you have poise or not. Sometimes it is very difficult to keep your poise or composure if you are angry or upset, but if you are a strong person, you can do it.

Discussion questions:

- Have you ever seen someone lose their poise?
- What would it be like to lose your composure during a game?
- Do you think keeping your poise will help you concentrate?
- Can you think of another word that starts with P that means the opposite of poise? (Answer: panic)

Class

Definition: Great style or quality

Teaching point: If you have class, people will recognize it. If you are lucky enough to win a game, you don't taunt, boast, or brag. If you lose, you don't make excuses or blame others. Those are examples of class.

Discussion questions:

- What are some things you can do after winning a game that show class?
- What are some things you can do after losing a game that show class?
- Can you show class in the way you dress?
- How can you show class by the way you treat people?

Loyalty

Definition: Being faithful to a person, country, idea, or conduct

Teaching point: If you are part of a team, school, community, or family, you should be faithful to them. Surround yourself with people you can count on and who can count on you.

Discussion questions:

- What does "You can count on me" mean?
- What or whom should you be the most loyal to?
- How can you be loyal to your teammates?
- Can you be loyal to something or someone you don't like or don't agree with?

Unselfishness

Definition: Being generous and thinking of others

Teaching point: Always try to make someone's day a little better. When playing a game, think about being a good teammate and being unselfish with your encouragement. Remember, if you get a lot of awards, it is due to your hard work, but a lot of people supported you.

Discussion questions:
- When you help someone else achieve, how does that make you feel?
- Give me an example of something you can say to someone that would show you are an unselfish teammate.
- Does a team work better together if no one is concerned about who gets the glory?

Caring

Definition: To be concerned about others, to look after others or take charge of their welfare

Teaching point: The world could use more caring people. To be concerned about the feelings of others is a noble characteristic.

Discussion questions:
- Can you show your parents you are a caring person? How?
- How can you show your teammates?

Enthusiasm

Definition: Great interest in and excitement about something

Teaching point: Find things about school and sports that excite you and then give 100 percent of your effort. If you love what you are doing, it is easy to be enthusiastic about it.

Discussion questions:
- Think of things you are enthusiastic about.
- Do you find it hard to be enthusiastic about some things? Can you do anything to overcome that lack of enthusiasm? Could you set goals?
- Can you be too enthusiastic about something? What could happen?
- Find something to be enthusiastic about this week. See if enthusiasm spreads.

Courage

Definition: The quality of mind and spirit that helps one to take risks or face hardship with confidence and firm control of oneself

Teaching point: There will be many things you will want to do in life. But sometimes you need the courage to "give it a try." You also need courage to develop a strong character.

Discussion questions:
- Why does it take courage to develop a strong character?
- What does "courage of your convictions" mean?
- Does it take courage to be the best you can be in your favorite sport?
- Does it take courage to enter a race even though you know it will be tough?

Confidence

Definition: A good feeling about yourself and your abilities

Teaching point: Sometimes we are not so confident because we think we might fail. If you work hard and prepare, your confidence will grow and you won't be afraid of failure; you will look at it as just a temporary setback.

Discussion questions:
- Does having confidence mean you will be the best at something?
- How can you gain more confidence?
- Can you have confidence in yourself and still lose or fail at something?
- Can you have confidence in your team? How can your teammates have confidence in you?
- Do you have confidence that your everyday behavior is promoting good character?

Commitment

Definition: A pledge or obligation to follow a certain course of action

Teaching point: If you want to be as good as you can be at something, you have to be committed to it. Hard work and commitment will help you reach your goals.

Discussion questions:
- Do you know how to set goals? Should you write them down or keep them as dreams in your head?
- How can teammates be committed to a team?
- How can you be committed to school?
- Take time tonight to write down one dream or goal and think about how to reach it.

Discipline

Definition: Controlled behavior formed by training or work that tends to mold a specific skill

Teaching point: When others fall behind or forget what's important, use your discipline to continue moving toward your goal.

Discussion questions:
- How is self-discipline different from the discipline your parents or teachers use with you?
- Do we all have self-discipline? What makes us want to use it?
- How do you discipline yourself to achieve a physical skill like shooting a basket?
- How do you discipline yourself to work toward good grades in school?
- If you discipline yourself, will others have to discipline you?

Principles

Definition: A statement or set of statements describing the way someone acts or behaves

Teaching point: Decide what is important to you in life, then use your guiding principles to achieve those things you have identified. Keep your life in balance, and always remember your principles and how they help you accomplish your goals.

Discussion questions:

- What are some of the ways we believe people should act when they are playing a game?
- What is one of the most important principles everyone should agree on when playing a game?

This chapter offers 19 words to teach and discuss. However, you can come up with others. Let students choose other focus words and lead them as they discuss these new words. Continue adding to this list by watching the behavior of your classes to determine concepts they might need to discuss.

REFLECTION SCENARIOS

The following team talks are modeled on real-life situations that students can easily relate to. Students will understand these scenarios because they are situations they most likely have been in and will be in again. By constructing ways to handle these scenarios, students will be better prepared for the specific conflict and thus handle it in a positive way. Use these scenarios the day after you introduce a focus word. These scenarios can be discussed as a class, or each team can be given a scenario for a quick discussion within the team.

Sportsmanship and Fair Play

A fourth-grade class was playing volleyball in PE one day. The blue team had won the first two games, and it was obvious that the green team was beginning to get frustrated. They were starting to yell at each other for making mistakes. The class played a third game, and once again the green team lost. As the blue team celebrated, a member of the green team ran up to the teacher and said in an angry voice, "These teams aren't fair!" Another player from the same team yelled, "They cheated!"

Discussion Questions

- Were the players on the green team who yelled at their teammates and complained to the teacher helping their team?
- How do those people look to the rest of the class?
- What could they have done to help their team?
- If your team just lost three games in a row, what could you do to show that you were a good sport?

Caring

The Saints basketball team played for the regional championship. The winner of the game advanced to the state high school tournament. The team that lost was done for the year. It was a great game that came down to the final seconds. The Saints were down by one with three seconds left when Mark, the Saints' point guard, was fouled while going up for a jump shot. The foul gave him two shots at the free throw line, which meant he could pull his team ahead by one if he made them both. The crowd went wild as Mark calmly stepped up to the line. He missed the first one, but he still had a chance to tie the game. The second shot rolled around the rim twice and bounced out. The Saints lost the game and were out for the season. Mark fell to the floor in disappointment. John, Mark's teammate, put his arm around

Reflection scenarios discussion on pp. 37-38 adapted, by permission, from D.R. Glover and L.A. Anderson, 2003, *Character education: 43 fitness activities for community building* (Champaign, IL: Human Kinetics), 55-56.

Mark and did everything he could to help him feel better. Phil, another Saints player, walked by Mark and gave him an angry look.

Discussion Questions

- How do you think Mark felt when he missed both free throws?
- How do you think Phil made Mark feel when he gave him a dirty look?
- What do you think John was saying to Mark to make him feel better?
- Would you rather have Phil or John on your team? Why?
- Now think to yourself (don't share your thoughts with your teammates): Who are you more like, Phil or John?

Humility

Your class just finished running a mile in physical education class. Sarah and Jake were the first to finish. Sarah ran around yelling, "I won. I won. I came in first place!" As people finished, she quickly told them her time and that she was the first to finish. Jake, on the other hand, ran back and began cheering on his classmates without mentioning a word about finishing first.

Discussion Questions

- What are some words that describe Sarah?
- What are some words that describe Jake?
- Would you rather have Sarah or Jake on your team?
- Think to yourself (don't share your thoughts with your teammates): Who are you more like, Sarah or Jake?

CHARACTER EDUCATION FITNESS ACTIVITIES

The following activities reinforce character education concepts while developing fitness and strength. You can use them during your team-building unit, or they can serve as a team warm-up any time. All of the activities should be done in teams of five to eight students.

Character Cup Stack

GRADES

3–12

EQUIPMENT

- For each team: twelve buckets with character education words and a number from 1 through 12 printed on them. Your school cafeteria and custodians are good sources for five-gallon buckets that work well for this game.
- Building blueprints for each team. Create these blueprints ahead of time, showing different patterns in which the buckets could be stacked.

DESCRIPTION

This team builder is great fun and combines team communication skills with team planning. The objective of this challenge is to build various pyramids with the buckets.

1. Designate a starting area and place the buckets stacked in two columns of six in this area. Designate a finish area about 20 feet (6 m) away where the students will build the pyramids. Designate the construction office, which could be a hoop or a mat (see figure 2.1).

2. Let each team (no more than eight per team) determine who will be builders and who will be construction managers. For example, in a team of eight, six of the students will be builders and two will be construction managers.

3. Give the construction managers, who must stay in the construction office, the construction blueprints. When the six builders are ready, the construction managers yell stacking instructions to the builders according to the blueprint.

RULES //////

- Construction managers may not touch builders or buckets.
- Construction managers must stay in the construction office.
- Construction builders may move only one bucket at a time to the construction site.
- When giving instructions, construction managers must call each builder by his or her first name and use the character education word printed on the bucket.
- Construction managers may not use the terms *line*, *top*, *front*, or *behind*.
- Students may not call teammates by their last names or use put-downs.
- If a team breaks one of these rules, they must return the buckets to the starting area.

VARIATIONS //////

- The construction manager uses only the character education words to describe the buckets. When the manager calls out a word, the builder must give the word's definition before picking up its corresponding bucket.
- The construction manager uses only the bucket number to designate the buckets.
- Set a time limit for construction.
- The construction manager uses math equations to designate buckets. For example, use bucket 2 × 5 − 1 (bucket 9).
- Increase the distance between the starting area and construction area.
- Construction managers call out a different way to move from the starting area to the construction area each time a builder moves a bucket.

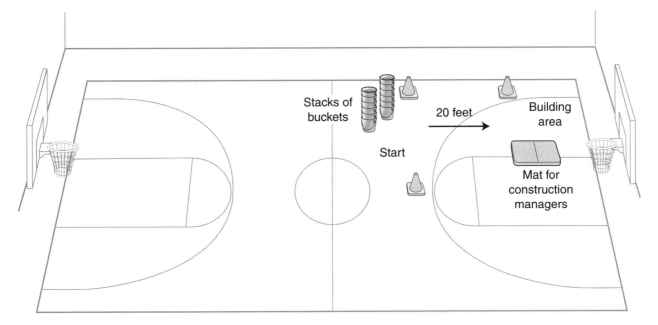

Figure 2.1   Setup for Character Cup Stack.

Activity adapted, by permission, from D.R. Glover and L.A. Anderson, 2003, *Character education: 43 fitness activities for community building* (Champaign, IL: Human Kinetics), 147-151.

|||||||||||||| **Integrity Tower** ||||||||||||||||||||||||||||||||||||||||||||||||||||||||||||||||

GRADES //////

1–8

EQUIPMENT //////

- Four sets of beanbags with character education words, such as respect, character, sportsmanship, judgment, pride, and integrity, printed on them (The beanbags can be purchased from the Gopher Sport catalog. You can look it up at www.gophersport.com to see what these beanbags are.)
- One folded gym mat per team
- Two gym scooters per team
- Three spot markers or bases per team

DESCRIPTION //////

Students work together to build a tower using the character education beanbags and to transport them in relay fashion to the building site. This activity enhances physical fitness and teamwork. You can also help students understand the importance of sound values by discussing with them what it takes to build an integrity tower and pointing out that they can use these same building blocks to shape their own character.

1. Set up the equipment in the gym according to figure 2.2. The character education beanbags, teammate one, and the folded mat should be located at station one at one end of the gym. Use the bases to designate stations two through four. Set up station two with a scooter and teammate two halfway between the half-court line and station one. Teammate three waits with a scooter at station three, which is located on the half-court line, and teammate four waits at station four, which is located between station three and the other end line. The building site is located on the opposite end of the court from station one.

2. The team should plan together in a huddle what order the beanbags will be delivered. On your signal, teammate one places one of the character education beanbags on the folded mat and pushes the mat to station two.

3. When teammate one arrives at station two, teammate two takes the character education beanbag, sits on the gym scooter, and transports the block to teammate three, who is waiting at station three.

4. Teammate three takes the beanbag from teammate two and transports it by the second gym scooter and delivers it to teammate four, who is waiting at station four.

5. When the beanbag arrives, teammate four takes it and sprints to the building site and starts constructing the integrity tower.

6. After handing off a beanbag, the teammates return to their original station traveling back the same way they came and wait for the next beanbag. Teammate one, who pushes the folded mat back and forth several times, will get the best workout. The team that builds the six-beanbag tower quickest wins the relay.

VARIATIONS ||||||

- Add other items, such as a cone, ball, or rhythm stick, to the construction materials for the tower. Label these dishonesty, cheating, and greed. Ask students to watch what happens when they try to include these items in the tower. Ask them the following questions: Is it easier or more difficult to build an integrity tower with these values?

- Use different methods to move the beanbag from station to station. Use different locomotor movements or different vehicles, such as pulling a tire with the beanbag on it or doing a forward roll or swinging on a rope. Be creative.

- Rotate teammates through the stations so that every child gets a chance to build a tower.

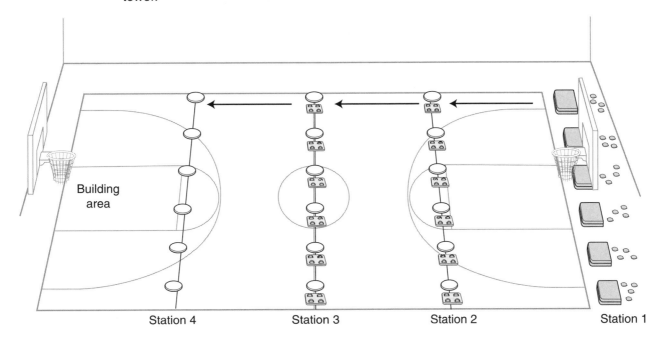

Building area

Station 4   Station 3   Station 2   Station 1

Figure 2.2   Setup for Integrity Tower.

Activity and diagram adapted, by permission, from D.R. Glover and L.A. Anderson, 2003, *Character education: 43 fitness activities for community building* (Champaign, IL: Human Kinetics), 91-92.

|||||||||||| **Character Education Treasure Hunt** ||||||||||||||||||||||||||||||||||||||||||

Respect
10 Push-ups

Figure 2.3 Sample card for Character Education Treasure Hunt.

GRADES //////

K–8

EQUIPMENT //////

- Thirty-six index cards in different colors, six cards per color. List a character education term and an activity on each card (see figure 2.3). Use the character education words listed in this chapter or make up your own character cards with other terms.
- Cones, beanbags, mats, poly spots—enough to hide 36 cards
- Six boxes or buckets

DESCRIPTION //////

1. Hide all 36 cards around the gym—under mats, pins, balls, bases, poly spots, and so on. This increases the excitement and requires teams to remember where other teammates have looked.

2. Place the six boxes or buckets in the middle of the gym. Divide the students into six teams, and assign each a bucket or box. Also assign each team a color to match the color of the cards. Assign one student from each team the role of the hunter.

3. On your signal, the teams jog around the perimeter of the gym. On the second signal, the hunter ventures away from the team in search of a character education card while the rest of the team keeps jogging. When the hunter finds a card with the right color, he or she calls the team to that spot, and everyone performs the activity on the card.

4. The hunter places the card in the team's bucket and rejoins the team, which has continued jogging around the gym. When the hunter rejoins the team, a new hunter ventures forth and looks for a new card, and the process continues. The game ends when all six teams find all their colored cards and place them in the bucket or box. It would be great to hear the teams yelling to the hunter, "We need Respect! Find Respect!"

Activity and diagram adapted, by permission, from D.R. Glover and L.A. Anderson, 2003, *Character education: 43 fitness activities for community building* (Champaign, IL: Human Kinetics), 89-90.

Chapter 3

Team Building

*T*eam building is the cooperative process that a group of individuals uses to solve both physical and mental challenges. While using this process and solving the challenges, the group learns how to share ideas, to praise and encourage one another, to physically and emotionally support one another, and to slowly start becoming a team.

The difference between team building and other cooperative programs is that groups participating in a team-building exercise must pay a price if they fail. The price may be starting over from the beginning or having one or two members of the team start over. When a team fails, it has two options: reorganize and begin again or quit. A team that has pride won't quit. In my years of team building, I have noticed that very few teams give up when the going gets tough. Team building can teach a community, a family, a workforce, or a sports team to reorganize and persevere.

For much more detailed information about team building and lots of activities, see *Team Building Through Physical Challenges,* Glover and Midura, Human Kinetics, 1992; *More Team Building Challenges,* Glover and Midura, Human Kinetics, 1995; and *Character Education,* Glover and Anderson, Human Kinetics, 2003. These are excellent resources for learning how to introduce and conduct a team-building unit.

This chapter provides team-building challenges for you to try with your classes. The students in the St. Mary's University (Winona, Minnesota) graduate program developed many of these challenges.

Egyptian Pyramid

GRADES

6–12

EQUIPMENT

- One rubber band
- Eight pieces of string about 10 inches (25 cm) long per group
- Six cups
- Stopwatch

DESCRIPTION

Teams must transfer six cups from the starting line to the finish line 15 feet (4.5 m) away, supporting the cup with only the strings and rubber band. At the finish line, they stack the cups into a pyramid. The equipment is located at the starting line. The strings are in a pile next to the rubber band and a vertical stack of six cups. This is a timed challenge.

RULES ||||||

- You may not touch the cups with your hands.
- You must use all eight pieces of string.
- The string may not touch the floor.
- Cups will start standing upside down in one pile going vertical.

STRATEGIES FOR SUCCESS ||||||

One possible solution: The team ties the strings to the rubber band, then pulls the strings to stretch the rubber band and slip it around the cup. The group lifts the cup from the stack and carries it to the finish line to start building the pyramid with three cups on the bottom, two in the middle, and one on top.

VARIATIONS ||||||

- Do not time the challenge for younger students.
- Add obstacles between the starting line and finish line to make transporting the cup more difficult. For example, students must step over a rope or duck under a high-jump bar.
- Make the strings longer to make the exercise more difficult.

|||||||||||| Carpet Slide ||||||||||||||||||||||||||||||||||||||||||||||||||||||||||||

GRADES ||||||

5–12

EQUIPMENT ||||||

- One board, 8 feet long (2.5 m)
- One jump rope for each group member
- One carpet square
- One bamboo pole
- Two tires
- One cone
- Stopwatch (optional)

DESCRIPTION ||||||

Group members must move a carpet square from its starting position, going under and around obstacles, to the finish line using an 8-foot-long (2.5 m) board and jump ropes. The task is mastered when the carpet square crosses the finish line. Label distinct starting and finish lines and side boundaries (see figure 3.1). Place the jump ropes and board at the starting line. Place the carpet square 2 feet (60 cm) from the starting line inside the boundary. Make a bridge by supporting the bamboo pole on the tires. Place the cone between the bridge and the finish line.

RULES ||||||

- Group members may not step within the boundaries.
- Group members may not touch the board after it crosses the starting line.
- Group members and equipment may not touch the bridge or cone.
- No one should call others by their last name or use put-downs.
- If a rule is broken, the group must start over.

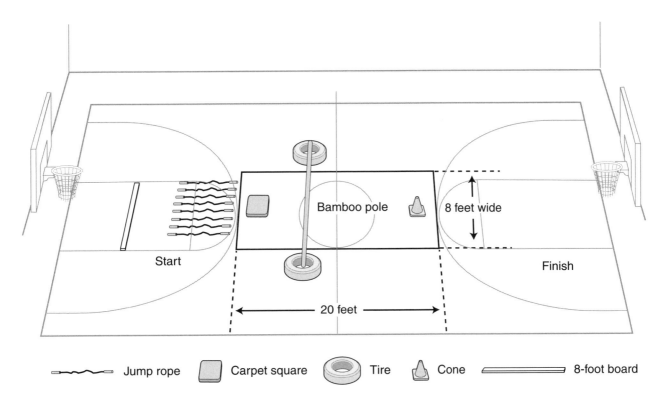

Figure 3.1   Setup for Carpet Slide.

STRATEGIES FOR SUCCESS ||||||

All group members manipulate the ropes (tied to the board) in order to place the end of the board against the carpet square and push the carpet square to the bridge. Group members push the carpet square under the bridge. They then lift the board over the bridge and place it onto the carpet square. The carpet square must then circle the cone once and proceed to the finish line.

VARIATIONS ||||||

- Add more obstacles to increase the difficulty.
- Widen or narrow boundaries and shorten or lengthen the ropes according to the height of the group members.
- Increase the height of the bridge.
- Push other objects such as a beanbag, football, or tire through the obstacle course.
- Impose a time limit, or challenge teams to beat their own time record.

|||||||||||| **Easter Egg Retrieval** ||||||||||||||||||||||||||||||||||||||||||||||||||||||||

GRADES //////

5–12

EQUIPMENT //////

- At least five beanbags
- One tire
- One large ball
- Participants' shoes

DESCRIPTION //////

Students perform this challenge on half a basketball court or outdoors. All team members throw their shoes into the perimeter. The group must maneuver itself from outside the activity area to the large ball in the center being held by the tire. The tire is the Easter egg basket (see figure 3.2). The group must suspend the ball in the air without using their hands or arms. Everybody in the group must be touching the large ball at all times. Once the ball is suspended, the group must move around and collect all the beanbags (Easter eggs) in the activity area without bumping into any of the shoes. No one is allowed to speak. The challenge is completed when the ball has been suspended and all the Easter eggs have been placed in the tire with the large ball covering them.

RULES //////

- If a group member touches the ball with the arms or hands, the group must start the challenge over.
- If the ball touches the ground, the group must start the challenge over.
- Everyone in the group must remain in contact with the ball until they return it to the tire. If anyone loses contact, the challenge starts over.
- If a team member hits a shoe, the challenge starts over.
- If anyone in the group moves out of the activity area, the challenge starts over.

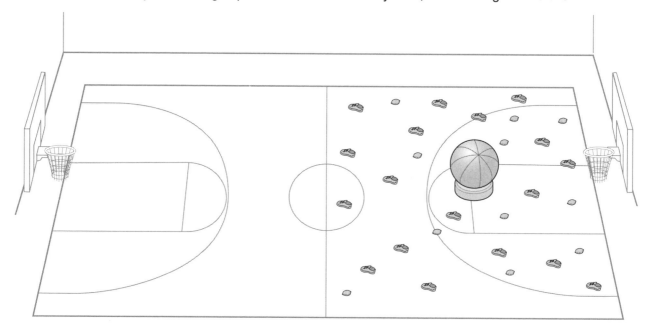

⬭ Beanbags   👟 Shoes

Figure 3.2 Setup for Easter Egg Retrieval.

- If a team member throws a beanbag into the egg basket or drops a beanbag, the challenge starts over.
- If anyone speaks, the challenge starts over.

STRATEGIES FOR SUCCESS //////

There is one solution to this task. However, the most significant aspect of this exercise is the participants' inability to speak, which controls team members who might ordinarily take charge of a challenge. Students can point to spaces they want to move to, or prior to the challenge the team could plan signals like stamping or clapping to indicate a move.

VARIATION //////

Use beanbags in two different colors and assign a color to each team. Let the teams race each other to see who can put the most eggs in their basket.

Twirl-a-Lot

GRADES //////

2–12

EQUIPMENT //////

- One 20-foot-long (6 m) jump rope
- Stopwatch (optional)

DESCRIPTION //////

All group members (I recommend groups of six to eight) must pass through the barrier (a rope being twirled by two players who must pass through the twirled rope) from one side to the other without touching it. Group members must pass between the twirlers as quickly as possible. The challenge is mastered when all group members have passed from one side of the barrier to the other without touching it. You will need a large working area, such as a gymnasium, to accommodate twirling the long jump rope. The twirlers will need to practice turning the rope because this will be crucial to the group's success. The group must also figure out how to change twirlers so they can also pass through the barrier.

RULES //////

- All group members must pass from one side of the barrier to the other.
- No one but the twirlers may touch the barrier.
- All group members must pass between the twirlers.
- If a group member touches the barrier or passes around the twirlers, then that person and *all* group members who have already successfully passed through the barrier must go back.
- The group members may use no last names or put-downs.

STRATEGIES FOR SUCCESS //////

There are two possible solutions. The group may solve the challenge as individuals or as a team. If the group decides to solve the challenge as individuals, then each person takes his or her turn passing through the barrier. Most groups will run into problems with this approach. In most cases, someone will touch the barrier or will not know when to pass through it as the rope is twirling. The best solution is for the group to work together. The entire group can pass through the barrier at the same time. To be successful, the entire group must stand close together shoulder to shoulder and on the signal run through the barrier.

VARIATION //////

Time the group or set a time limit, such as one minute, 30 seconds, or 10 seconds.

Great Mountain Climb

GRADES

4–8

EQUIPMENT

- Ten small cones
- Six orange cones
- Six blindfolds
- Four folding chairs
- Five tennis balls
- Two gym mats
- Six jump ropes

DESCRIPTION

In this challenge, every member on the team works with a partner. Students start at the base of the mountain (starting line) and make their way to the summit of the mountain (finish line) by zigzagging through pairs of cones and without dislodging boulders (tennis balls). The three boulders are tennis balls on top of the larger orange cones and two boulders on top of the folded gym mats. Pairs are connected by holding onto a rope. One person in each pair is blindfolded, and his or her partner serves as the guide as they make their way up the mountain. The course includes two caves constructed by resting a folded gym mat across two chairs and balancing a tennis ball "boulder" on top. Pairs must pass under the caves. The course also includes sets of cones the participants must navigate through (see figure 3.3). The challenge is mastered when all pairs have reached the summit without dislodging any of the boulders or knocking any balls off the orange cones.

RULES

- Both people in the pair must hold onto the rope with their hand. If one drops the rope, that pair must start over at the beginning of the challenge.
- One person in each pair must be blindfolded at all times. If the blindfold comes off, that pair must restart from the beginning.

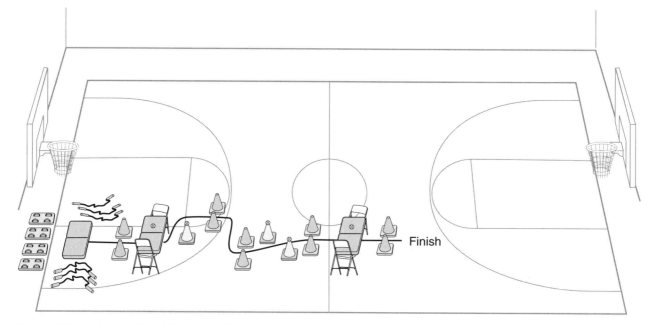

Figure 3.3 Setup for Great Mountain Climb.

- If one of the partners causes a boulder (tennis ball) to fall, that group must start again at the beginning.
- Participants must go through the "mat caves" by traveling under the mats.
- Students may not call each other by their last name or use put-downs.

STRATEGIES FOR SUCCESS ||||||

- To meet this challenge, students must communicate effectively. Moving slowly is also a good strategy.
- Teachers should check the folded mats periodically to see that they remain firmly on the chairs. They should station themselves next to the caves in case a mat collapses onto a student.
- Students must communicate with the blindfolded climber at all times.

VARIATIONS ||||||

- Use a longer rope with three or four teammates connected to the same rope.
- Don't use the blindfolds.
- Once the entire team has climbed the mountain, switch roles within the pair and travel back to the base of the mountain.
- Set up the course in any fashion that fits the needs of your classroom.

✳||||||||||| Island Hopping ||||||||||||||||||||||||||||||||||||||||||||||||||||||||||||||||||||||||||||

GRADES ||||||

10–12

EQUIPMENT ||||||

- Twenty-five carpet squares or poly spots (six should be of a different color)
- Twenty-five age-appropriate curriculum questions (at least 10 should be of a higher degree of difficulty)
- Map of islands
- Stopwatch

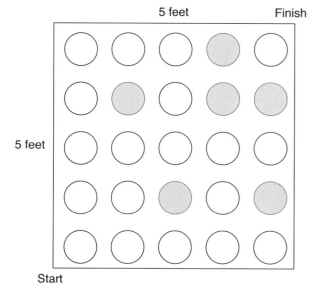

Figure 3.4   Setup for Island Hopping.

DESCRIPTION ||||||

Set up the 25 poly spots in a square on the floor, five spots wide by five spots long. Designate the spot in one corner as the starting point; the finish is the spot in the opposite corner. Surround the finish spot with three colored spots, and scatter the remaining colored spots throughout the pattern (see figure 3.4). When students stand on a colored spot, you will ask a more difficult question. Students will answer a question when standing on most bases; however, you can select up to four free bases that won't require answering a question. You will have a map of these islands. Team members may progress across the dots by correctly answering questions. Wrong answers cause the student who has progressed the farthest to start again at the beginning. The challenge ends when all the team members, including the team leader, reach the finish.

RULES ||||||

- The team chooses a leader.
- The leader sends out team members from the starting point no more than one base at a time and no more than one teammate per base.
- The teacher asks a question to the team member who just moved. Every question must be answered in thirty seconds.
- When a team member moves to a colored base, the teacher asks a more difficult question. The team has 30 seconds to confer and help the team leader to answer the question.
- A correct answer to a regular question or a more difficult question gives the team a chance to advance to another base.
- An incorrect answer results in the teammate who has advanced the farthest returning to the starting point. This player cannot help answer a question until two more questions have been answered successfully.
- If a base does not have a question associated with it, the team leader can send a teammate to a bordering base. This process can be continued until the team reaches a base with a question on it.
- When a team member reaches a base once occupied by a teammate, the teacher asks a new question for that base.
- The team leader must also advance to the finish base by answering questions. Conferring with the team is always allowed.

STRATEGIES FOR SUCCESS ||||||

The team should try to find an easy path to the goal (the path with the fewest number of colored spots). The best way to help students meet this challenge is to tell them the topic of the following day's activity the night before so they have time to study it.

VARIATIONS ||||||

- If a team member answers a question incorrectly, he or she is out of the game. The team with the most members who finish, wins.
- Allow more time for answering questions.
- Allow players to use their textbooks for one turn.

|||||||||||| Bucket Battle Quest ||||||||||||||||||||||||||||||||||||||||||||||||||||||||||||

GRADES ||||||

3–12

EQUIPMENT ||||||

- One gym scooter for each team member
- Five large unfolded mats
- Six to twelve curriculum word or phrase cards (subject area) depending on team size
- One or two small buckets
- Prizes to place in the island bucket (optional)

DESCRIPTION ||||||

Two teams race to see who can transport all team members across the river to the island and find the prize in the bucket first. Teams may send players across the river (across the gym floor on a scooter) after correctly answering curriculum questions you have provided on cards (see figure 3.5). Students use charades to act out the situation or word on the card. Students may also play the game using questions, word simulation, or word association. The task is completed

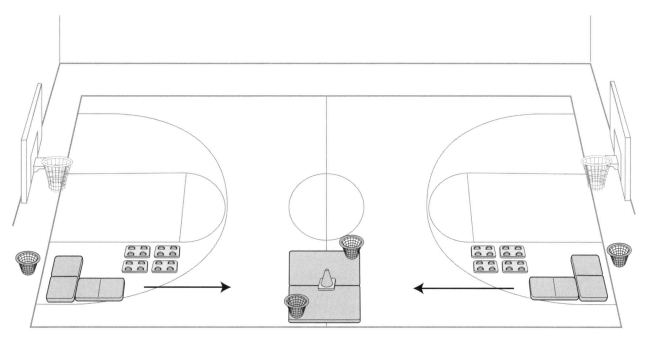

Two-team setup

Figure 3.5   Setup for Bucket Battle Quest.

when all team members have reached the island (mat) and answered the final question, which will allow them to gain their prize in the bucket.

RULES //////

- Each teammate takes a card from the team's bucket and acts out a word or situation without using oral or written communication to try to get the team to correctly answer the question. The team must decide who will act out the first question and continue to decide the rotation. If teammates answer the question correctly, the actor is allowed passage to the island on a gym scooter.

- Even though a team member gains passage, he or she may decide to stay with the team rather than go to the island because once a person crosses to the island, he or she may not try to guess any more answers. Therefore, teams may decide to send two, three, or even all the teammates at one time to the other side of the river.

- Participants must steer their scooters straight, travel at a safe speed, and not crash into others while crossing the river on their gym scooter.

- Team members cannot attempt the final quest of gaining the prize until all team members are safely on the island. The team then has to decide who will act out the final question.

STRATEGIES FOR SUCCESS //////

Students should devise strategies for efficiency. For example, they must decide if team members should go one at a time to the island or if everyone should go at once. Skill in acting games or being a good guesser in acting games is important in solving this challenge, as well as knowing the subject matter on the curriculum cards.

Sample charades scenario: It is the night of December 25, and the Americans have been forced to retreat from yet another battle. The Americans find themselves trapped on one side of the Delaware River and the only way out is to get across the river before the Hessians wake up.

Answer: Washington crossing the Delaware

VARIATION //////

To make this game easier, let the team pick its best charade performer for each scenario.

River Crossing

GRADES

3–12

EQUIPMENT

- Six PVC tubes about 6 feet (1.8 m) long
- Two tires
- Two cones
- Six scooters
- One tunnel
- One marble
- One small box
- Stopwatch (optional)

DESCRIPTION

Six participants must move a marble within the PVC tubes from one side of the river to the other without touching it, making sure it passes through the tunnel and finally putting it in the box (see figure 3.6). All participants must cross the river in their boat (scooter).

To set up the course, make two islands by placing the cones on top of the tires. Make sure that all positions are one tube length apart (from start to island one, from island one to the tunnel, and so on). This challenge is complete when the marble is in the box and all team members are on the opposite side of the river.

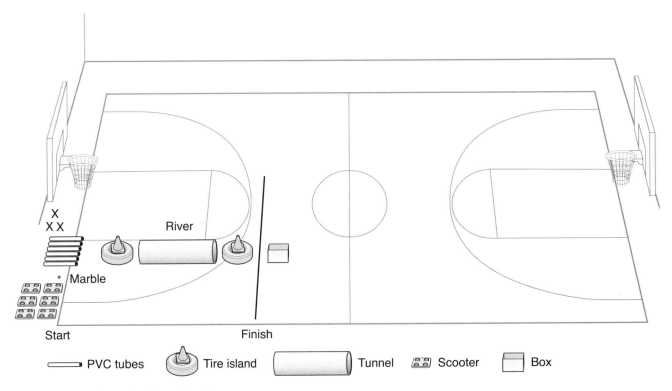

Figure 3.6 Setup for River Crossing.

RULES ||||||

- No one may touch the marble after it has been placed inside the first tube at the starting point.
- Team members may only move the marble while it is inside a tube.
- The marble must pass through each tube.
- Team members may not transport the tubes by scooter while the marble is in it.
- The marble must pass through the tunnel.
- The marble must land in the box on the other side of the river.
- All participants and tubes must end up across the river. Students may paddle across using their hands.
- No one should call teammates by their last name or use put-downs.
- If any of the rules are broken, the challenge starts over.

STRATEGIES FOR SUCCESS ||||||

Station a participant at each end of the river with tubes, two people in the tunnel with tubes, and a person on each tire with a tube. Pass the marble from the start through the tubes to the box. All participants then roll themselves and their tubes to the other side of the river on their scooters.

VARIATIONS ||||||

- To make it easier, eliminate the tunnel.
- To make it more difficult, do not allow anyone to touch the river with any part of his or her body.
- Time the challenge.

|||||||||||| **Shipwreck** |||||||||||||||||||||||||||||||||||||||||||||||||||||||||

GRADES ||||||

1–12

EQUIPMENT ||||||

- Eight scooters
- Ten poly spots
- Two 4-by-6-foot (1 × 2 m) mats
- Twenty cones

DESCRIPTION ||||||

One of your teams (six to eight on a team) is aboard a ship from Europe headed to the United States. The other team has left the United States for Europe. During a terrible storm the vessels became shipwrecked in the middle of the ocean. Both ships have lost their global positioning system (GPS), sonar, and all communication equipment. Each team's mission is to figure out how to reach their destination *before* the other team reaches theirs. The challenge is completed when every team member successfully crosses the ocean *with their equipment* and reaches their destination (see figure 3.7).

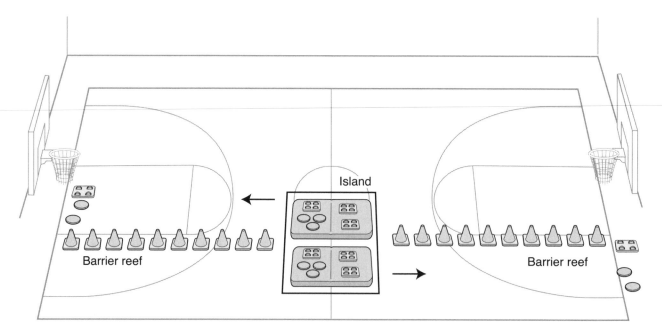

Figure 3.7 Setup for Shipwreck.

RULES ||||||

- If anyone touches the ocean (floor) with a part of his or her body or clothing, the equipment he or she is using must remain at that spot but the teammate must return to the start; however, another team member may use it. If equipment hits the barrier reef, it is also lost.

- The scooters may not be whipped across the floor at any time, nor can they be used as skateboards. To do so results in the team's loss of the scooter.

- Once a team member makes it to his or her destination, he or she may not touch the water. If that happens, the team member must start again on the other side of the ocean.

- All equipment must end up at the team's destination.

- Do not call team members by last names or use put-downs. If this happens the person that committed the infraction must start over.

STRATEGIES FOR SUCCESS ||||||

- Turn the scooters over and use them as floating stepping stones.

- Unfold the mat, then use it and the poly spots to make a trail to walk across the water.

- Keep the mat folded and put it on top of the scooters to make a raft using poly spots to cover hands as they push.

- Use the scooters as individual lifeboats and the poly spots as oars to pull the students along.

VARIATIONS ||||||

- To make the challenge easier, add more scooters and poly spots. You can also add ropes and plungers and tire islands in the ocean.

- To make it more difficult, explain that when the storm occurred, some people were injured. Assign various injuries to different group members. For example, one person can't use an arm, and another team member is blindfolded.

IIIIIIIIIIIIIIIIII **Meteor Shower** IIIIIIIIIIIIIIIIIIIIIIIIIIIIIIIIIIIIIIIIIIIIIIIIIIIIIIIIIIIIIIIIIIIIII

GRADES ||||||

6–12

EQUIPMENT ||||||

- Five tennis balls
- Five bases or poly spots
- One scooter

DESCRIPTION ||||||

Mark an area of the gym 30 to 40 feet (6 to 12 m) for space travel. An astronaut sits on a scooter at one end of space (activity area), and a rocket launcher (teammate who pushes him or her) stands behind the astronaut. Both are behind the starting line. Five team members line up on bases or poly spots along one side of the playing area (see figure 3.8). These teammates face the playing area and each throws a tennis ball to the astronaut as he or she flies through space. You can make the playing area longer if you need to accommodate more team members. Teams meet the challenge when the rocket launcher propels the astronaut through space to the finish line in one push, and the astronaut catches all five meteors during flight. Use this challenge only after you have provided instructions on scooter safety and appropriate throws.

RULES ||||||

- The rocket launcher must remain behind the starting line.
- The astronaut must not touch the floor with any body part, and the scooter must remain three-fourths of the width of the area (15 feet [4.5 m]) away from the throwers. You can use cones to show where the boundary is, or just estimate.

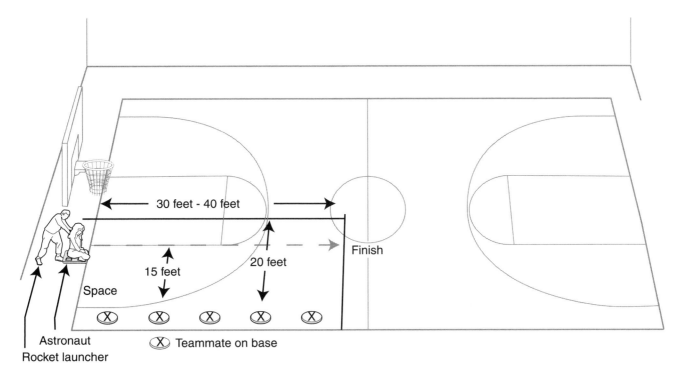

Figure 3.8   Setup for Meteor Shower.

- The astronaut must catch the balls with his or her hands.
- If the astronaut fails to catch all five meteors or any of the other rules are broken, players rotate and attempt the challenge again. The rocket launcher becomes the new astronaut, and the astronaut goes to the first base. Each teammate on a base moves one base closer to the starting line. The base closest to the start becomes the new rocket launcher.
- The astronaut must travel to the finish line with just one push. If he or she doesn't reach the finish line, the team must try again, even if the astronaut has caught all the meteors.
- No one should call others by last names or use put-downs.

STRATEGIES FOR SUCCESS ||||||

This is a fairly difficult challenge; however, with some practice every team will eventually be able to solve it. The rocket launcher cannot push the astronaut too hard or the astronaut will not have time to catch the balls because he or she will be moving too fast. An easy underhand toss by the teammates on the bases is the best way to deliver the ball. Each tosser must toss after the astronaut has successfully caught and tucked away the previous ball.

VARIATIONS ||||||

- Add barriers in space, such as cones, that the astronaut may not touch.
- Increase or decrease the number of balls.
- Make the challenge more or less difficult by using different equipment for the meteors (e.g., beanbags or yarn balls).
- Place throwers on both sides of the playing area.
- Alter the distance from the throwers to the astronaut.
- Use larger or smaller balls to make the challenge more or less difficult.

|||||||||||| Treasure Cave ||||||||||||||||||||||||||||||||||||||||||||||||||||||||||||||||||||||||

GRADES ||||||

1–6

EQUIPMENT ||||||

- Six cones
- Three yardsticks
- Two long jump ropes
- Treasure pieces (beanbags, tootsie rolls, tennis balls, etc.—enough so that there will be one for each team member)
- Four gym scooters
- One blindfold
- Two deck-tennis rings
- Stopwatch (optional)

DESCRIPTION ||||||

Each group member must travel down the dark mine shaft one at a time to retrieve a piece of treasure. The mine shaft consists of a series of yardsticks placed horizontally across two cones (see figure 3.9). Each blindfolded explorer must pass through this "mine shaft" without touching its toxic walls. Team members must be careful not to roll over fingers when using the gym scooters and be careful not to push a blindfolded team member into objects on the course. The challenge is mastered when every group member has gone down the mine shaft,

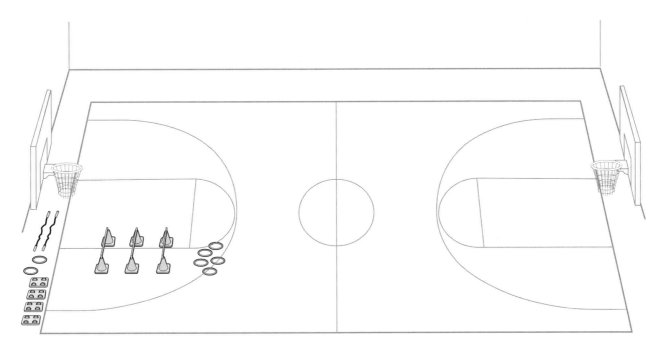

Figure 3.9   Setup for Treasure Cave.

retrieved a piece of treasure, and returned to the surface of the Earth without touching the walls of the shaft.

RULES ||||||

- Team members may not touch the cones or the yardsticks. If they do, they must return to the Earth's surface.
- Explorers must go through the mine one at a time and remain blindfolded while in the shaft.
- Teams must use three different methods of moving through the tunnel to complete the challenge.
- Team members may go through the shaft in the same manner as another team member as long as the team uses three different methods.

STRATEGIES FOR SUCCESS ||||||

The team members may arm crawl, crab walk, lie on their tummy on a gym scooter and push with the feet or pull with the hands, and use a rope to pull themselves or other members of the team through the shaft. The team may also keep one team member in the treasure cave to help other teammates. Team members must decide who will use which method to travel through the shaft. Teammates must move slowly and carefully and only move when given a specific direction. Teammates who are waiting to go through the mine shaft must decide who will give the blindfolded teammate directions.

VARIATIONS ||||||

- Attempt the task without the use of verbal communication.
- Place obstacles in the mine shaft.
- Time the challenge.
- Lengthen the challenge course.

⫼⫼⫼⫼⫼ **Magic Bases** ⫼⫼⫼⫼⫼⫼⫼⫼⫼⫼⫼⫼⫼⫼⫼⫼⫼⫼⫼⫼⫼⫼

Jimmy Gehm, a physical educator in Missouri, designed this challenge. He was kind enough to share his favorite team builder with me and allow me to use it here.

GRADES ⫼⫼⫼⫼

K–12

EQUIPMENT ⫼⫼⫼⫼

- One 12-inch (30 cm) poly spot for each team member making the journey, plus two extra poly spots
- Stopwatch (optional)

DESCRIPTION ⫼⫼⫼⫼

Set up the poly spots in a figure-8 pattern, but with one end open (see figure 3.10). Designate an entrance spot and an exit spot. The age, size, and motor development of your students will dictate the distance between spots. The spots should be no farther away from each other than one big step, and younger children may need them closer together.

Team members hold hands and, starting at the entrance dot, travel through the figure-8 pattern without speaking or touching the floor. When teammates need to communicate, they must do so without talking. Magic Bases is completed when all group members successfully complete the pattern and exit from the last base.

RULES ⫼⫼⫼⫼

- The team must travel the figure-8 route while holding hands. If anyone disconnects hands at any time, the whole group must start over.
- There may be no more than four feet on any one poly spot at the same time.
- Team members may not touch the floor.
- No last names or put-downs can be used.
- If a team member breaks a rule, the group must start over.

STRATEGIES FOR SUCCESS ⫼⫼⫼⫼

The team must take it slowly and help one another balance on the bases or poly spots. When hopping or stepping from base to base, students must be careful not to pull the person next to them off of his or her base. When the team meets at the crossroads of the figure-8, they must figure out how to communicate, without speaking, how they will cross paths. One group could hold their arms low so that the lead group can step over, or one group could allow the rest of

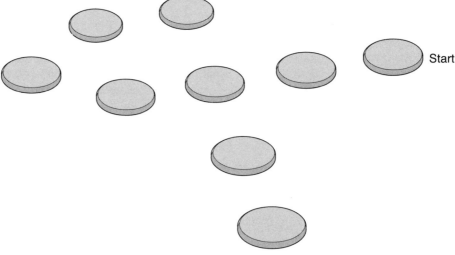

Figure 3.10   Setup for Magic Bases.

the group to pass under their connected arms. The team will have to take turns passing over or under the arms of their teammates at the intersection of the figure-8.

VARIATIONS ||||||

- Designate one base as the speaking base. Students may not talk until they reach that base. This allows each student to provide input during the challenge.
- Time the challenge.
- Once the first person in line reaches the fifth base, the team must figure out how to make that person the last person off the course or last in line.

Activity adapted, by permission, from D.R. Glover and L.A. Anderson, 2003, *Character education: 43 fitness activities for community building* (Champaign, IL: Human Kinetics), 128-129. This activity was created by Jimmy Gehm.

|||||||||||||| **Whole World** ||||||||||||||||||||||||||||||||||||||||||||||||||||||||||||||||||||||||||||||||||||

GRADES ||||||

1–12

EQUIPMENT ||||||

- One large cage ball 36 to 42 inches (91-107 cm)
- Two tires
- Stopwatch (optional)

DESCRIPTION ||||||

This challenge was featured in *Team Building Through Physical Challenges*. It is one of the most popular challenges I teach at workshops and in-service presentations. Here, however, I have changed it to make it even more fun.

The group stands around a cage ball sitting on a tire (see figure 3.11*a-b*). A second tire is on the floor about half the length of the gym away. The challenge is mastered when the students move the cage ball from the first tire, transfer it across the gymnasium, and balance it on the second tire. The students must move the ball from tire to tire a total of four times, each time

a

b

Figure 3.11   Setup for Whole World.

accomplished differently than the previous trips. This is an introductory challenge, but, as in all challenges, group discussion should precede any physical attempt. Group members must use their problem-solving skills to figure out the first attempt and make the solution understandable to all.

RULES ||||||

- The cage ball cannot touch the floor.
- Group members may not touch the cage ball with their arms or hands.
- The group must move the ball from tire to tire a total of four times; each time using a different transferring method.
- If the team breaks a rule, they must start again from the tire the ball was on before the rule was broken.
- No last names or put-downs can be used.

STRATEGIES FOR SUCCESS ||||||

This challenge has a multitude of possible solutions.

- The students can lift the ball by squeezing it between their bodies and moving collectively as a team.
- The team could move the ball using their chests and tummies.
- Team members can lie on the ground in two parallel lines similar to railroad tracks. As the ball moves along the "human tracks," the team members must get up and move to the front of the line to add more track. When the ball gets near the tire, at least four group members should help position the ball onto the tire.
- Two people could crawl forward on their hands and knees with the ball on their backs. The rest of the team could keep it balanced as the crawlers move forward.

VARIATIONS ||||||

- Add obstacles for the team to maneuver around while transporting the ball.
- Time this activity.

Activity adapted, by permission, from D.R. Glover and D.W. Midura, 1992, *Team building through physical challenges* (Champaign, IL: Human Kinetics), 39-43.

|||||||||||| **Team Balance Board** |||||||||||||||||||||||||||||||||||||||||||||||||||||||||||||||||||||

GRADES ||||||

1–12

EQUIPMENT ||||||

- One team balance board (You will have to make this yourself, as I have not been able to get it commercially made.)
- Two 6-foot-long (1.8 m) 2-by-4 inch (5 × 10 cm) boards and wooden 2-inch-by-4-inch-by-4 inch stabilizers under each board with a wooden fulcrum in the center for stability. (Essentially, you are making two 6-foot low balance beams crossed at the center and connected to each other at the fulcrum.)
- Four mats

DESCRIPTION ||||||

This challenge is fun for all ages and requires physical support from teammates. Place two low balance beams so that they cross each other in the middle. You can also use two boards with stabilizers under each of the four ends. Place mats along the length of one of the boards on both sides, right up against the fulcrum. The objective of this challenge is for team members to exchange places and move to a new number as designated by the teacher (see figure 3.12).

RULES //////

- Once everyone is on the team balance board, they may not touch the ground again until the challenge is complete.
- While exchanging places, everyone must pass over the center X. Teammates may not step across to the other board.
- No one may use put-downs or use last names.
- If a team member breaks a rule, the team must get off the team balance board and start again.

STRATEGIES FOR SUCCESS //////

The team must communicate when getting onto the boards to determine the best way to distribute their size on the top board. They must move slowly and must physically assist one another when changing positions. The team must plan an orderly rotation that prevents everyone from moving at once.

VARIATIONS //////

- The team must pick up a beanbag or other object at the opposite end of the board and return it to their original position.
- Each team member must carry an object during the exchange.

Figure 3.12   Team members must cooperate and communicate when using the team balance board.

Teaching Movement and Skills

As a physical education teacher, you know that teaching movement and skills is at the heart of your job. That's why part II features skill-building activities that are sure to complement your existing curriculum.

Many physical educators are timid when it comes to teaching rhythms and dance, but it can be great fun for the students—and for you—with the activities presented in chapter 4. Rhythms and dance can help your students be more creative, confident, and fit.

Chapter 5 covers gymnastics and tumbling, a subject area that is fun to teach and offers students lasting physical education benefits. The activities in this chapter involve progressive balance, tumbling, and creative play experiences that build students' strength and coordination in a cooperative context.

In chapter 6 you'll find activities that teach and reinforce important sport and fitness skills. Teaching a sport skill such as hurdling or shooting a layup might seem intimidating if you have little experience with that sport. However, any teacher, regardless of knowledge and experience with a particular sport, can teach a sport skill effectively by breaking it down into parts and using key words. Not only is this an effective way for you to teach, but it's also an effective way for students to learn. The activities in this chapter teach skills using this approach. I've found it to be a very successful method over the years, and I think you will, too.

Chapter 4

Rhythms

So often we as educators look for new and creative methods for delivering the latest material. There is nothing wrong with that. We should always be on the lookout for ideas that can benefit our students. However, we must be careful not to throw out something just because it is old. Let's not make the mistake of believing that "old" might mean "not good anymore." Many older techniques and methods, if delivered properly, are as useful and effective today as they were when they first came onto the educational scene.

Such is the case with rhythms. Folk dances, square dances, and line dances have long been the most prevalent way to teach rhythms, and it's still the case today. Dances are fun and easy to teach. There are dances appropriate for every age level, and if you present them with enthusiasm, the kids will eagerly participate. This chapter provides dance activities, but before you begin the dances, try a couple of games and activities to introduce rhythm concepts. A few of my favorite rhythm activities are included at the beginning of this chapter.

RHYTHM ACTIVITIES

These activities are beneficial to students because they familiarize them with a beat. When the students become comfortable with a beat or rhythm, moving to it becomes much more fun. Any skill is more fun if you can relax while practicing it.

Teacher's Beat

GRADES

K–6

EQUIPMENT

Drum or tambourine (optional)

DESCRIPTION

1. Children spread out and sit on the floor, each child in his or her own space, or sit grouped in teams.
2. Clap or drum a beat for them, such as the following:

CLAP   CLAP-CLAP

slow   quick-quick

Now ask the children the following questions and practice each one before moving to the next question:

- Can you clap this rhythm with me?
- Can you move your arms around you in time to the beat, reaching out and using all the space around you?
- Can you use large arm movements, keeping time with the beat? Tiny arm movements?

3. Speed up the beat while the children continue making patterns with their arms. Then slow the beat, and use the term "slow motion" to change speeds. Ask the following questions:

- Can you make up arm patterns using this beat and combining speeds?

  clap-clap-clap—clap—clap—clap-clap-clap-clap

  clap—clap—clap

- Can you add moving body parts—moving your arms and head, legs, hips, and so on?

4. Now let the children make up their own movement patterns using different speeds. Ask them to try the following:

- Make a movement pattern with a partner or in a group. How can the movement pattern be changed? Can you make up a dance with a partner or your group?
- Moving to the beat while using small equipment, such as a wand, pin, rope, ball, chair, bench, and box (Encourage students to be creative and try many different movement combinations.)
- Making up their own beats and combining the beat with different speeds and different pieces of equipment

  clap-clap-clap—clap   and   clap—clap—clap

5. Now let's add two more elements to our rhythm activities: level and direction. Ask the following question:

- Can you make up a movement pattern using different speeds, levels, and directions?

  clap-clap-clap-clap   and   clap—clap—clap

  (high level)   (low level)

  (forward)   (backward)

  (_____ Movement Pattern _____)

|||||||||||||| Rhythm Name Games ||||||||||||||||||||||||||||||||||||||||||||||||||||||||||

GRADES //////

K–6

EQUIPMENT //////

- CD player
- Music

DESCRIPTION //////

1. You can have a lot of fun making patterns using names for rhythm. For instance, Pat gets one beat; Bobby gets two beats; Julia gets three beats. Ask students to say these names and clap them:

Pat	Bob/by	Ju/li/a
clap	clap-clap	clap-clap-clap

Ask the following questions:

- Can you try it at different speeds?
- Can you clap it at different levels?
- Can you clap it using a different force on each name?
- Can you clap each one in a different direction?
- Can you combine some of these activities?
- Do you have other ideas?

2. Ask students to "walk" the names, taking a step with each syllable.
3. Add movement challenges by suggesting different locomotor movements, directions, levels, speeds, and force, such as the following:

- Gallop backward
- Run sideways
- Leap high
- Hop low
- Slide heavily
- Crawl lightly

4. Give each child a chair or a bench. Ask them to make up a pattern using names and the chair.

Bobby   Julia

sit stand   skip around

5. Put the students in groups and ask each group to make up a dance using names. Remember to include different locomotor movements, directions, speeds, and levels.

Creating Patterns With Music

GRADES

K–6

EQUIPMENT

- CD player
- Music

DESCRIPTION

Creating and expressing to music is a great way to learn rhythms. Any song with a strong beat or a strong rhythm works well for expressive rhythm. Use different types of musical expressions from the minuet to the latest pop tune. Different music suggests different movements; for example, the minuet brings out swinging, swaying, graceful movements. One of my classes' favorite songs is "Irish Washerwoman." This song has a heavy beat that children love to move to. It, as well as other fast folk songs, suggests skipping.

With the children spread out in their own spaces, listen to the music and ask the following questions:

- What does it remind you of? Does your body feel like moving when you hear it?
- Can you clap the rhythm?
- Can you move your arms in the space around you, keeping time to the rhythm?

- Can you use your arms and head and keep time to the rhythm?
- Can you move your arms, head, and hips to the rhythm?
- Can you sit and move your legs to the rhythm?
- Lie on your back, and put your legs in the air. Can you keep time to the rhythm with your legs?
- Can you move your whole body to the beat?
- Can you make a movement pattern to this song? Try it with a partner. Try making up a dance in groups.

Talk the Walk

GRADES

K–6

EQUIPMENT

None

DESCRIPTION

1. There is a natural rhythm between our mouths and feet, so in this exercise, ask students to put together different locomotor movements and say them as they do them. For example, have the children walk and say "walk," hop and say "hop," and skip and say "skip."

2. Next have students combine movements and changes in speed, such as "walk—walk" (slow) and "hop-hop-hop" (fast).

3. Add changes of direction, levels, and force to vary the possibilities. For example, "Slide—slide" (slow at a medium level), "twirl-twirl" (fast at a higher level), "skip—skip—skip" (slow at a medium level), then repeat the sequence going in the opposite direction.

4. To further vary the activity, try this while throwing and catching a ball, jumping a rope, or working with a partner or group.

LINE DANCES

After teaching basic rhythm activities, you can teach the children a few dances. I have enjoyed teaching folk dances such as the shoemaker's dance, Danish dance of greeting, how do you do, my partner, and the children's polka to kindergarten through second grade classes. And I have taught classics like glow worm, bingo, cotton-eyed Joe, bleking, and lottist Todd to grades three through six.

I learned the line dances presented here at a "Devotion to Motion" workshop put on by Mike Wagner, physical education director of South Washington County schools in Minnesota.

Rosie's Slap

GRADES

2–8

EQUIPMENT

- Recording of "Uptown Girl" by Billy Joel
- Tape or CD player

DESCRIPTION

Jon Carver-Carlson and Gary Saunders presented these dances at the "Devotion to Motion" workshop in 1987.

1. Hitchhike thumb over right shoulder, two counts; over left shoulder, two counts; to the right side, two counts; to the left side, two counts.
2. Roly-poly (same motion as an official's traveling call in basketball), raise arms over right shoulder high, two counts; over left shoulder high, two counts; right side low, two counts; left side low, two counts.
3. Touch right hand on left shoulder, touch left hand on right shoulder.
4. Slap right hand on right rear, slap left hand on left rear.
5. Jump forward three times, quarter turn right on fourth jump (for a variation, crisscross legs three times before turning).
6. Repeat sequence.

The Wanderer

GRADES

5–9

EQUIPMENT

- Recording of "The Wanderer" by Dion
- CD or tape player

DESCRIPTION

1. Tap right toe to the right side and back, repeat (four counts).
2. Tap left toe to the left side and back, repeat (four counts).
3. Tap right toe to the right side, touch right toe behind left foot, tap right toe to the right side, bring right toe up in front of left leg (four counts).
4. Do grapevine to the right with a quarter turn to the right on the fourth beat (four counts).
5. Walk back, left, right, left, and a quick right left (four counts).
6. Repeat sequence.

Cotton-Eyed Joe

GRADES ||||||

6–12

EQUIPMENT ||||||

- Recording of "Cotton-Eyed Joe"
- CD or tape player

DESCRIPTION ||||||

1. A line of girls faces a line of boys. Students join hands with the person standing directly in front of them (see figure 4.1).
2. Moving to boys' right, the students do heel-toe-step-close and then to the boys' left, heel-toe-step-close.
3. Now partners turn away from each other and walk in a small circle back into place. While making their circles, they do three heel-toe-step-close steps ending with a stamp-stamp-stamp.
4. Partners again move away from each other, do four side steps—boys to right, girls to right—and return to their partner doing four more side steps.
5. Upon returning to their partner, they hook right elbows and swing doing three step-close steps ending with a stamp-stamp-stamp.
6. Repeat.
7. One variation is for partners to move past each other in the fourth step, pairing with the next person in line. The boy on the end runs to the other end to the free girl.

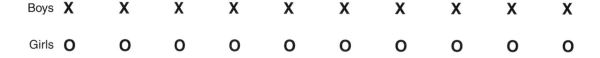

Boys X   X   X   X   X   X   X   X   X   X

Girls O   O   O   O   O   O   O   O   O   O

Figure 4.1 Setup for Cotton-Eyed Joe.

Tennessee Wig Walk

GRADES ||||||

3–8

EQUIPMENT ||||||

- Recording of "Tennessee Wig Walk"
- CD or tape player

DESCRIPTION ||||||

1. A line of girls faces a line of boys, as in Cotton-Eyed Joe. Tap left foot out front, to the side, and behind, then take a small jump backward with both feet.
2. Repeat with the right foot (don't forget the jump).

3. Do a schottische step starting with the left foot—one-two-three-hop—and a schottische step with the right foot—one-two-three-hop.

4. Do a step-hop with the left foot and a step-hop with the right foot, pause, and then stamp-stamp (the stamps are just a stamp left and stamp right).

5. Repeat the whole dance.

6. As a mixer, the boys move ahead to the next girl on the schottische step. Girls take smaller schottische steps so that the boys can catch up.

Bouncer

GRADES

5–9

EQUIPMENT

- Recording of "Hey, Look Me Over"
- CD or tape player

DESCRIPTION

1. Pat lightly with the palms knee-belly-clap-clap. Repeat eight times.

2. March eight counts.

3. Jump eight counts.

4. Jump two times in each direction starting to the left.

5. Hop four times on each leg.

6. Hop two times on each leg.

7. March one-two-three-four.

8. Repeat sequence.

Chapter 5

Gymnastics and Tumbling

You may wonder why I have included a tumbling section. It is because I could not stand this activity when I was in school. I was a tall, skinny geek and did not have the strength to pull off some of the stunts I saw my classmates do. However, after attending a movement education workshop it quickly became my favorite unit to teach, and I think my students have enjoyed it also.

Teaching gymnastics and tumbling is important in developing students' strength and coordination. Learning to put weight on the hands and arms through such simple stunts as animal walks opens up a new world of movement.

A lot of physical education teachers make students perform routines in front of their classmates. I have allowed my students to create their own routines and practice them *with* the class rather than in *front* of the class. Please consider this option because many of your students are, I assume, much like me and do not have great ability in gymnastics.

INTRODUCING BALANCE EXPERIENCES

It is important to introduce balance experiences first in the gymnastics unit because not only do they require different ways to support the weight, but they also require creative thinking about how the body can move from balance to balance.

During the gymnastics unit, take two class periods just to work on balance, and try to give the students as many creative experiences with balance as possible. After the children come into the gym and find their own space, move on the road, or report to their teams, start the balance lesson this way.

Balance Lesson

GRADES

K–6

EQUIPMENT

Music if desired

DESCRIPTION

While the students are in their space, ask them the following questions to lead them through activities that progressively enhance their balancing skills. Give students ample time to create and practice their answers.

- Today we are going to find as many body parts as we can to balance or support us. Who can name some body parts that could help to balance us? (Possible answers are knee, shoulder, elbow, head, feet, arms, tummy, and seat.)

- Now, who can balance on any four of the parts we named? A combination of any four? How many different combinations can you find?
- Can you make your four-point balance at a low level, a high level, and a medium level?
- Let's make a rule—we will stretch whichever parts we are not using for support. We will call these stretch balances. Let's try to make a stretch balance on three parts. Who can make up a good one?
- Who can figure out three three-point balances and put them into a pattern? Go from one balance to another without stopping.
- Who can figure out five two-point balances? Does anyone have a knee–toe combination? Can anyone do Johnny's two-hand balance?
- How many can balance on the tummy? On the seat? Can you stretch your feet and arms? Make a high balance on your seat? A low balance?
- Can you find other parts of your body that can support you?
- Can you make a pattern of balances? Use a four-point, a three-point, and a two-point balance, and flow from one balance to another without stopping. Remember to stretch the parts you are not using.
- Try all of these activities with a partner. Can you and your partner find a good way to help each other balance?
- Let's get into groups of five. Can your group find a way to help each other balance while only nine body parts touch the ground?
- Which groups can balance on nine total parts (see figure 5.1)? Six? Five? Which group can balance on ten parts?
- Can you and your partner figure out ways to balance so that one partner supports the other?

Figure 5.1　A group of kindergarteners tries to help each other balance while only nine body parts touch the ground.

After working on balance skills, begin combining those skills with locomotor movements. This goes a long way in helping students plan their movements as well as helping them develop their creative-thinking skills.

- Let's skip in the big space to music. On my signal, freeze in a two-point stretch balance position.
- Let's combine three different locomotor movements with three balances. When the music starts, pick a locomotor movement. When I clap my hands, change locomotor movements. When the music stops, do a three-point stretch balance. Let's do this two or three times until your pattern is perfected. Now I will let the music go and you put the locomotor movements and balances together any way you want. Let's try five minutes of practicing your pattern.
- Post a chart of locomotor movements on the gym wall. Encourage the children to make different patterns using as many combinations of locomotor movements and balances as they can. Here are some of the patterns you might see: run—stop—one-point balance; gallop—jump—stop—two-point stretch balance; skip—leap—stop—three-point stretch balance.
- Ask students to try these patterns with a partner.

INTRODUCING CREATIVE TUMBLING

After the students have had time to practice putting together locomotor skills and balances, they are ready for creative tumbling experiences. A good way to introduce young students to tumbling is through animal walks. These walks help the children develop bilateral coordination and, like the balance lesson, lets them practice putting weight on their hands.

Animal Walks

GRADES

K–4

EQUIPMENT

Two mats for every three or four students

DESCRIPTION

Scatter sets of two mats lined up end to end around the gym. Locate three or four children at each set of mats. I usually group team members together on a mat and situate groups from the same team close to each other.

Instruct the children to line up at one end of the mat. Name an animal, and ask the children to show you how they think the animal moves. Many times a student comes up with the correct movement, and you can challenge the rest of the class to imitate that movement. If they don't come up with the correct walk, show them how to do it.

When one student is halfway down the mat, the next student may start. The students can perform the walks down the mat and back to their starting point. Perform the animal walks in this sequence.

- *Puppy walk.* Student walks on hands and toes.
- *Puppy with hurt paw.* One back foot never touches the mat because the puppy hurt it. This puppy walk requires arm strength and coordination. Try it for a short distance with the front paw hurt. This is more difficult than the puppy walk, so attempt it after the student has had experience with the puppy walk.
- *Puppy with two hurt paws.* Get into puppy walk position (hands and toes on the ground). Now lift one hurt back paw off the ground and the opposite front paw off the ground. Ask

students if they can move forward with just two good paws. This is very difficult and students may be able to make just one or two steps before losing balance.

- *Bunny hop.* Squat down, placing hands on the mat between the knees and in front of the feet (see figure 5.2). Move hands forward about 12 inches (30 cm), then hop forward with two feet. (Demonstrate and say the sequence with a bit of rhythm: Front paws, then back paws—front paws, then back paws—front paws, then back paws.)
- *Frog jump.* Squat in a position similar to the bunny walk. Then jump forcefully upward, landing on the feet in a squatting position. During flight, the arms extend upward, then touch the mat when landing.
- *Mule kick.* Walk forward, place hands on the mat, and kick the feet backward into the air. Challenge the students to see if they can kick higher each time.
- *Bear walk.* Balance on all fours with the hands and toes positioned just like in the puppy walk. Move the right hand and right leg forward, then the left arm and leg. Continue walking forward—right side, then left side—right side, then left side.
- *Crab walk.* Balance on the hands and feet with the tummy facing upward. Try walking forward and backward in this manner.
- *Turtle walk.* Spread the arms and legs wide in the push-up position, then move forward.
- *Inchworm.* Stand up straight. Now reach down and place the hands on the ground in front of the toes. You may have to squat down to do this. Now walk the hands forward until the body is in the push-up position. Now, taking tiny steps and keeping the legs as straight as possible, walk the feet up as close as possible to the hands. Now walk the hands forward again, then the feet. Repeat the sequence down the mat.
- *Seal crawl.* Get into the push-up position—hands on the mat, but with the top of the feet rather than the toes touching the mat. Move forward using only the hands, dragging the back part of the body.

Try these walks backward, sideways, and in a circle.

Figure 5.2 Bunny hop.

‖‖‖‖‖‖‖‖‖ Creative Tumbling Lesson ‖‖‖‖‖‖‖‖‖‖‖‖‖‖‖‖‖‖‖‖‖‖‖‖‖‖‖‖‖‖‖‖

GRADES ‖‖‖‖

K–6

EQUIPMENT ‖‖‖‖

- One mat for every two students
- Music (optional)

DESCRIPTION ‖‖‖‖

The students are ready to discover or reinforce previous tumbling discoveries. At this point, you don't need to teach the students specific tumbling skills. However, when someone discovers the correct basic tumbling skill, break down the movement for the other children and praise the student for discovering the best way to do a roll or cartwheel.

Line up the children along the side of their mat as shown in figure 5.3. Lead them through the following questioning sequence.

- Can you walk across the mat?
- Can you walk back across the mat?
- Can you cross over and go back moving in a different way?
- Can you think of 10 different ways to cross the mat?
- Can you cross the mat a different way every time you hear the beat? (Teachers, if you can find the record "Childhood Rhythm Series, Album Two," by Ruth Evans, you can use the song "Elevators" for this question. During the song, a beat sounds 32 times at a steady interval. If you don't have the record, skip this question and just play music as students practice various skills back and forth across the mat.)

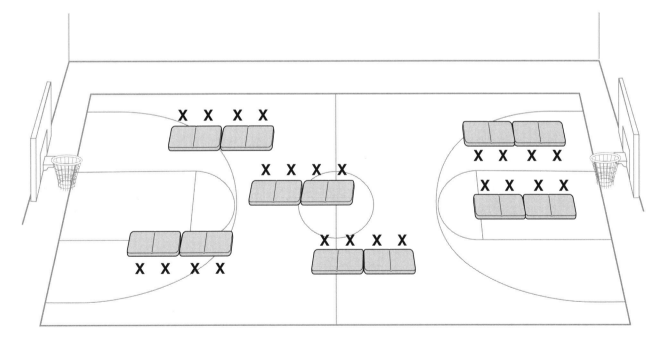

Figure 5.3 Setup for Creative Tumbling Lesson.

Soon someone will do a log roll across the mat. Stop the class and ask that person to show everyone the great way he or she has found to cross the mat. Ask the following questions:

- How many think they can do a log roll?
- Can you stretch your arms and legs?
- Can you roll straight?

Someone else may soon try a forward roll. Again, stop the class and ask the student to demonstrate the great way they have found to cross the mat. Ask the following questions:

- What touched the mat first? (Answer: hands)
- What did the hands and arms do to help you do this forward roll? (Answer: balanced and supported us)
- What touches the mat next? (Answer: head)
- What part of the head—the top, the front, or the back? (Answer: the back)
- What touches next? (Answer: shoulders—then back, hips, feet)
- Who thinks they can do a forward roll and do it in that sequence? Remember, don't let the top of your head touch the mat.

Let the children practice log rolls and forward rolls as you walk around and give individual help. After a practice period, ask the following questions, and allow more practice after each:

- We have been starting the forward roll from a squat. Who thinks they can start a forward roll from a balance?
- Who thinks they can start a forward roll after a jump-twirl?
- Now I will put the music on and give you time to find as many different ways as you can to start a forward roll.

Many of you will have children who simply cannot do a forward roll. Let them do a log roll instead while you are presenting them with the preceding challenges. If children fear doing a forward roll, do not force them to do it. Fear could cause injury—they can do all challenges with a log roll or a modified forward shoulder roll. Next ask the students to find ways to finish a forward roll. Ask the following questions, and allow a practice period after each:

- Can you finish your forward roll in a low-level three-point balance?
- How many can find a high-level balance?
- Let's try changing speeds during the roll. Can you change speeds during the beginning, middle, and end of your roll? Who thinks they can do that?
- Can you find three different ways to start your roll, perform your roll, and finish your roll? Remember, change speeds and balances.
- Try all of these creative problem-solving questions with the backward roll. (Go through the same beginning discovery questions as you did for the forward roll, then let students try different starting and ending balances or movements.)

Go back to finding new ways to cross the mat. Pretty soon a child will cross the mat using a cartwheel. Stop the class, go through the same questioning sequence. Then let the children practice. Many of the children will be very hesitant to try rolls or cartwheels. These children can add locomotor movements—leaps, twirls, hops, and so on—and use a log roll as their main tumbling move. Let the children attempt to solve these challenges slowly, and give extra help when necessary. The nice thing about practicing in this way is that everyone is working, so they are not watching each other. Children can progress at their own rate. Another great strategy (one that I did not use until the 1990s) is to allow mat partners to coach each other and give each other feedback.

Now it is time to let the students put locomotor movements, balances, and tumbling together into creative patterns. Let the students go the length of the mats now, combining locomotor movements, balances, and rolls. Tumbling can be fun and nonthreatening if you let students progress at their own speed and do not make them perform in front of their peers unless they want to show what they have made up.

INTRODUCING CREATIVE PLAY AND EXPLORATION

For preschoolers through second graders, a combination of free exploration and structured teaching is the best avenue for learning. If a learning environment is attractive and fun and has plenty of challenges and opportunities for creative movement, a child's natural curiosity will take over. Provide an area that includes objects to balance on, crawl through, run around, jump over, hang from, and jump off of. Then let the children take off. Children need to learn to try new things and have adventures. During the process of free exploration, a child develops balance, strength, agility, and self-confidence to a much greater degree than they do through structured learning only. Set up a play area once or twice during your tumbling and gymnastics unit.

If you have the time, equipment, and help to set up a play area, start the very young children with free exploration before introducing specific tumbling lessons. Then go back to the play area at the end of the unit. Too often we want to teach too much to young children. Free exploration, under your supervision, provides fun and an opportunity to learn. Here are ideas for your play environment. Remember, safety is a key component to your play area. Use plenty of mats and try to recruit parents or other volunteers to watch over the students.

Preschool–Primary Play Area

GRADES

Ages 3 to 8 years

EQUIPMENT

- High-jump and pole-vault pits
- Gymnastics crash pads
- Ladders
- Tables
- Wrestling mats
- Hoops
- Low balance beams
- Gymnastics high bar
- Gym mats
- Climbing ropes
- Large boxes
- Tunnels
- Benches
- Track awards stand
- At least three adult volunteers (parents, teacher aides, and so on)
- Music and player (optional)

DESCRIPTION //////

You cannot set up a play area that encourages skill and strength development without equipment. Your district has it hidden away somewhere—find it. It helps to have a good relationship with your principal, the facilities crew, the custodian, and the coaches.

- *High-jump and pole-vault pits.* The track coach has these stored somewhere, and won't use them until spring. Ask the coach, then have the district facilities crew deliver them to you. These pads are tall enough that a child could get hurt if he or she falls off them, so don't use them if you can't find gymnastics crash pads to place around them.
- *Crash pads.* In a basement or garage storage area somewhere in the district are the old gymnastics pads. In 1987, I found six of them and convinced my district to re-cover them. We still use them. These pads should be at least four inches thick.
- *Straight ladders.* Your custodian has one hanging somewhere in the back storage area. Ask him or her if you can use it. Check at the high school and middle school also. You may want to use two or three.
- *Low tables from classrooms.* You may only need two or three of these. Drape an old mat over the table, or surround the table with crash pads. Kids can jump off or crawl under them.
- *Wrestling mats.* Check around the district storage for old ones, if you don't have new ones available. Clean them up and use them in your play area.
- *Hoops.* You probably have a lot of these in your storage room.
- *Low balance beam.* You may already have one, or ask the gymnastics coach if you can borrow one or two. Also, look in district storage.
- *High bar.* If your school is old, there are probably floor clamps built into the gym floor. That means there is an old high bar somewhere—find it.
- *Climbing ropes.* If you have climbing ropes suspended from the ceiling, use them. I have allowed my kids only to hold on while I swung them. I did not allow them to climb.
- *Cloth or fabric tunnels.* These can be purchased at a low cost through a retailer that sells PE equipment, such as Gopher Sport or Sportime.
- *Benches.* These should not have a backrest. Check in locker rooms or the storage areas in the basements of older elementary schools that may have been the junior high or the high school at one time; they may have had benches in the locker rooms.
- *Track awards stand.* Again, ask your track coach.
- *Large boxes.* Appliance boxes work well; check with stores that sell appliances.
- *Gym mats.*

Find a time when you can set up your play area and use the equipment for two or three days straight. Then it can all go back where it came from. Leave it up and lock the gym at night. Or push it all to the side and set it up differently the next day. You will also have to find a time when the gym is not being used at night. Make your principal aware of your great plans and make sure he or she backs you 100 percent.

Set up your play area with safety in mind first. Then make skills and fitness a priority by arranging the equipment something like the setup shown in figure 5.4. Students can use the equipment in the following ways, among others:

- *Track awards stand.* Climb the stand and jump off different levels.
- *Climbing rope.* Hang and do limited swinging.
- *Hoops.* Crawl or jump through.
- *Pole-vault pad and high-jump pad.* Bounce on one pad or jump from one to another (only two on one pad at a time).
- *Tunnel.* Crawl through.

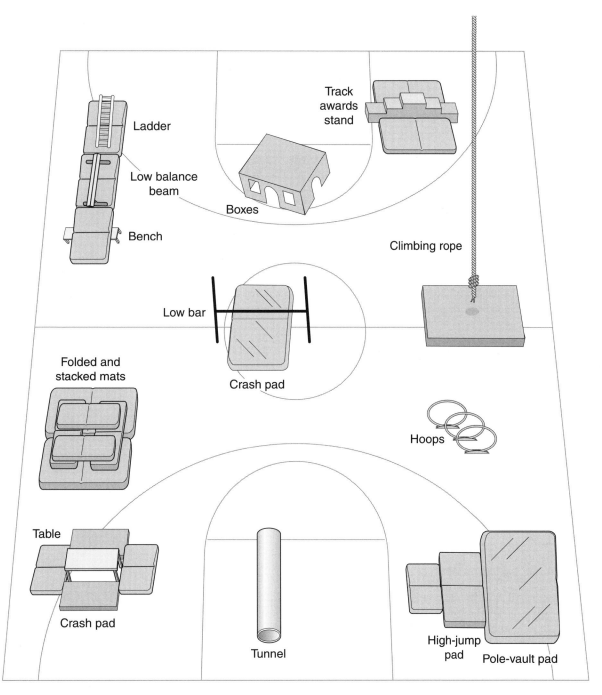

Figure 5.4   Sample setup for Preschool–Primary Play Area.

- *Table and crash pads.* Crawl under, climb over, and jump off table.
- *Folded and stacked mats.* Climb around and through.
- *Bench.* Walk on, jump off.
- *Low balance beam.* Walk on, jump off.
- *Ladder.* Walk on rungs or rail.
- *Boxes.* Crawl through.
- *Low bar.* Hang and do limited swinging.

When the children come to the gym, they will be very excited when they see the equipment. Here are rules they must agree to before you let them begin:

- When the music starts (optional), they may begin exploring the equipment. When the music stops, they must stop moving and sit down.
- They may explore with a friend or two but may not push or shove other people in order to use a station. They must use good manners and be courteous.
- They must visit every station.
- They must ask the teacher for help if they need it.
- They may hold onto the rope and hang from it or sit on the knot. They may swing, but only if an adult swings them.
- Only two students are allowed on the big jump pads at a time.
- Make sure no one is in your path before jumping off of anything.

Take the children around the gym and ask for ideas they could try at each station. Now station the adult volunteers where you think they can provide the most help. Put the music on and let the kids explore. Keep a sharp eye out for potential hazards. Your volunteers can help you take down the equipment and put it away.

Gymnastics Stations

GRADES

2–6

EQUIPMENT

- Flat ladders
- Flat benches
- Low balance beam or the following eight-foot-long (2.5 m) boards: 2 two-by-sixes (5 × 15 cm) and 2 two-by-fours (5 × 10 cm) (Wrap these boards in duct tape to prevent slivers.)
- Mats
- Music and player (optional)

DESCRIPTION

For older kids, use only the ladder, bench, and low balance beam or boards. The older kids take risks I am not comfortable with, and I doubt you and your principal would be either. Combine this equipment with the locomotor, balance, and tumbling skills we started this unit with. Figure 5.5 shows how I have set up my gym. You may have more ideas and different equipment. My stations worked as follows:

- *Station 1 (ladder—mat—mat).* Students can walk on or between rungs, walk on rails, or walk with one foot on a rail and one on a rung. Ask, "Can you combine a ladder walk with a roll, locomotor movement, and stretch balance? Can you make all the movements flow together?"
- *Station 2 (mat—bench—mat—mat).* Ask students, "How many ways can you use the bench? Who can do a vault? Who can combine a roll, vault, locomotor movement, and roll in a pattern?" Have students take turns sitting on the bench to stabilize it for other students.
- *Station 3 (mat—mat—bench—mat).* Have students come up with other creative ways to use the bench besides vaulting.
- *Station 4 (mat—low balance beam—mat).* Ask students, "Can you combine a locomotor movement with a roll and a balance on the beam?"

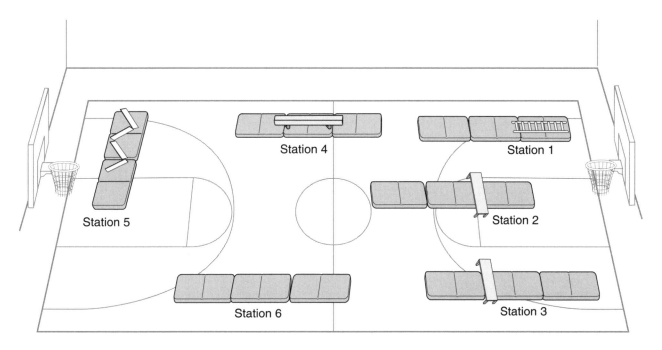

Figure 5.5   Sample setup for Gymnastics Stations.

- *Station 5 (boards—mat—mat).* Ask students, "Can you combine a balance, a roll, a loco-motor movement, and a balance beam walk on the boards?"

- *Station 6 (mat—mat—mat).* Have students combine skills. For example, "Can you combine two balances and two rolls?"

In this setup place three students or fewer at each station. You can rotate stations on a signal. On the second or third day you do this activity, ask the students to work longer at their favorite station and perfect a routine. Play music while the students use these stations. Music seems to encourage movement and creativity. Sometimes when students are waiting to use a station, they may do an impromptu dance.

If a student is hesitant or feels unsafe doing a forward or backward roll, then let them do two different balances or locomotor movements. Allow your more talented students to do cartwheels or walkovers.

Chapter 6

Sport and Fitness Skills

Many times we physical education teachers shy away from teaching certain skills, such as hurdling, running, throwing, or shooting a layup, because we might not have had much experience with that skill or we might think that the skill is inherently learned through a game or sport. But teaching skills is easy and fun—and necessary. The best way to teach a skill is to break it down into components and teach those components using language that the children understand. Then, give them opportunities to practice, practice, practice!

I have found that questions and challenges help students learn skills, so I have presented these activities along with the list of questions and challenges I present to my classes. You can use this method or not, but I have found that the students respond positively to it. In this chapter you learn how to teach the following listed skills. Remember to give students many opportunities for movement experiences while practicing these skills.

- Dribbling a basketball
- Pivoting
- Shooting a layup
- Running
- Hurdling
- Throwing
- Catching

BASKETBALL SKILLS

Playing basketball lead-up games or playing the game itself does not guarantee that a student will learn the skills involved in basketball. Therefore, the dribbling, shooting, and pivoting skills taught in this section are broken down so that even very young children can understand how to perform them.

IIIIIIIIIIIIIII **Dribbling** IIIIIIIIIIIIIIIIIIIIIIIIIIIIIIIIIIIIIIIIIIIIIIIIIIIIIIIIIIIIIIIIIIII

GRADES //////

K–8

EQUIPMENT //////

- One basketball for each student
- Music if desired

DESCRIPTION //////

1. The students should spread out in the gym and sit down in their own space, each child holding a ball. Demonstrate to the children how to hold the ball with their hand under the ball (see figure 6.1). The basketball should rest on the finger pads, not the palm.

2. Now show them how to "peel the peach" by closing their hand and popping the ball up. Do this several times, each time reminding them that they are peeling the skin off the peach. Ask, "Can you peel the peach?" The children should remain seated while attempting this. For kindergartners and first graders, you may want to use a smaller playground ball or volleyball.

3. Put your hand on top of the peach and let it drop to the floor, then peel it every time it bounces back to you. Ask, "Now can you do this?" Demonstrate, then let them practice. Ask, "What part of your hand are you using to dribble the ball?" (Answer: finger pads)

4. Show the students where the palm of their hand is. Let them try dribbling with the palm. Now make sure they know where the finger pads are and have them try dribbling the ball

Figure 6.1 The basketball should rest on the finger pads, not the palm.

Figure 6.2 Use the finger pads to touch the ball, but push it down with the hand and arm.

with the finger pads (see figure 6.2). Ask, "Which part of the hand did you like dribbling with the best?"

5. Vary and increase the difficulty by asking the following questions:

- Can you dribble while kneeling in your space?
- Can you dribble while standing up? Remember to use your finger pads!
- Now that we are standing, we have to push the ball a little harder. Who can keep using their finger pads to touch the ball but push it down with their hand and arm?

6. If you let everyone work at their own speed answering questions and practicing without paying attention to anyone else, the students will be involved and have fun. Try playing music while they practice. Here are more questions to help students improve dribbling skills.

- Can you dribble the ball using just your fingers? Now use your fingers and hand. Now use your fingers, hand, forearm, and whole arm.
- Who can dribble the ball and keep it at waist level? Can you walk and do this? Let's walk and dribble the ball at waist level. On my signal, who can change the way they move and still keep the ball waist high?
- Try dribbling the ball knee high. Remember, use your fingers. Can you walk and dribble it knee high? Who can run and keep dribbling knee high? Try it skipping and then sliding.
- How high can you dribble the ball without losing control? How low? Which is easier?
- Can you dribble fast at a high level? At a low level? How quickly can you change directions dribbling at a high level? Can you change directions more quickly at a low level?
- Let's see who can control the ball well. I want you to dribble in the big space, then on my signal, change direction and level. Let's see how many times you can change without losing the ball. Remember, you cannot touch anyone else.

- Change speed and direction on my signal. Change speed, direction, and level. Boy, that's a tough one. Who can do it?
- Let's add different locomotor movements to the dribbling moves we've tried. Can you dribble while skipping or galloping? This could be tough. I wonder who can do it?
- How slowly can you dribble; how fast can you dribble? Can you start with your slowest dribble and work up to your fastest? Try it the other way.
- Let's run our fastest while dribbling. Stop as quickly as you can on my signal.
- Get a partner and play follow the leader. You must do every movement the leader does, but both you and the leader must always dribble the ball. Who thinks they can do it?
- Let's try some of the moves we just tried again, this time using our nondominant hand. (For most children, this will mean using the left hand instead of the right. Consider starting all over with the left hand.)
- I have a difficult one. I bet no one will be able to do it. Who can walk and dribble the ball at a low level, without looking at it? Look at your friends.
- Let's try to change direction without looking. (You could try all of these dribbling challenges again asking the children to keep their eyes off the ball.)
- Do you have any more ideas? Try them.
- Can you find new ways to dribble? (This challenge will give the children a chance to explore. Here are some of the responses I've gotten in the past.)

- Dribble around and through the legs
- Dribble figures, such as triangles, squares, numbers, and names
- Dribble the ball as quickly as possible
- Dribble with different parts of the body, such as elbow, knee, wrist, and head

- Walk on knees while dribbling
- Hop, jump, and crawl while dribbling
- Jump or bounce body in time with the ball
- Dribble while moving in different ways
- Start the ball bouncing from the floor by hitting it with the fist

IIIIIIIIIIII **Pivoting** IIIIIIIIIIIIIIIIIIIIIIIIIIIIIIIIIIIIIIIIIIIIIIIIIIIIIIIIIIIIIIIIIIIIIIIIIIIIIIII

GRADES IIIIII

K–6

EQUIPMENT IIIIII

- One ball for each student
- CD player and a recording of the song "Seven Jumps"

DESCRIPTION IIIIII

1. While the students are sitting in their own space in the gym, take out a pretend hammer and nail and tell the students, "I want you all to pretend you have a hammer and nail. Now, let's nail our favorite foot to the gym floor. Let's pound a nail in the very top of our tennis shoe right between the big toe and second toe. Okay, everyone stand up and pound in your nail."

2. Now, demonstrate how you can move your other foot to open spaces, but you cannot move your favorite foot to another space. However, show them how the shoe with a nail in the toe can *pivot* around the nail. Let the students practice the pivot for a couple of minutes, then ask them the following questions (see figure 6.3):

Figure 6.3 Pivot and stretch.

- Who can pivot and stretch? Pivot and show me another stretch. (Students should stretch *away* from the pivot foot, like basketball players avoiding a defender when they have the ball and no dribble left.)
- I am going to clap my hands every three seconds. Can you do a pivot and stretch on every clap?
- Can you go from a high stretch to a low stretch, then back to a high stretch with every clap?

3. Tell the students, "Now let's try walking when the music starts. When it stops, I will clap three times. You try three pivots, one on each clap. Then when the music starts you choose another locomotor movement. We will repeat this sequence five times."

4. Play a recording of the song "Seven Jumps." This is a folk song that is older than I am. The music encourages running and skipping and is interrupted seven times by a series of beeps. Ask your students, "Who can run when the music is playing but pivot and stretch every time a beep sounds?" This exercise provides a good workout, and when the music is over, the students will have had a lot of pivot experience.

5. Now combine dribbling with pivoting. Repeat all the problem-solving pivot questions, adding the dribble. Tell students to pretend that someone is trying to steal the ball from them so they must stretch to hold it away from that person. Here are a few sample questions:

- When the music starts, dribble anywhere you want to in the gym. When the music stops, I will clap three times. Can you do three pivot stretches with the ball?
- Who can do this while running and dribbling?
- Who can do a jump-stop and then pivot?

6. Let the children practice pivoting around their nondominant foot also. You may or may not have to get out the hammer and nail again for the other foot.

IIIIIIIIIIIIII **Layup** IIIIIIIIIIIIIIIIIIIIIIIIIIIIIIIIIIIIIIIIIIIIIIIIIIIIIIIIIIIIIIIIIIIIIIIIIIIIIIIIIIIIIIII

GRADES IIIIII

K–8

EQUIPMENT IIIIII

- One basketball for each student
- Basketball baskets; the more the better
- Music if desired

DESCRIPTION IIIIII

1. With the students sitting in their own space, clap this rhythm:

   clap—clap-clap

   slow—quick-quick

   Clap this rhythm several times. Ask students to clap it with you, practicing it several times. Say, "The reason we are clapping this rhythm is because it is the rhythm needed in the last three steps of the layup." The students should be familiar with this rhythm before they create it with their feet.

2. Say, "Now stand up. Let's see if we can put this rhythm into our feet. Can you do it in your own space? If you are right-handed, make your first stamp on your left foot. If you are left-handed, stamp the first slow stamp on your right foot. I wonder who can do that?" (For the rest of these teaching questions, the questions are written for right-handed students for simplicity's sake.)

   stamp—stamp-stamp

   slow—quick-quick

3. Say, "Okay, now that you have the rhythm in your feet, let's see if we can move around the gym using this rhythm. Let's try walking the rhythm. If you are right-handed, your foot pattern will be left, right, left. Let's all try this several times to my call."

4. Say, "Now I wonder if we can go much faster. Let's try running this rhythm." Practice this several times. This lets the students ingrain the proper footwork and rhythm in their bodies.

Figure 6.4 Correct shooting position.

5. Now it's time to add a ball. On the first slow step, students dribble the ball. Then on the quick-quick they put the ball on the palm of their dominant hand. Say, "Let's pretend we are serving a tray of water glasses in a fancy restaurant. Hold the tray (ball) on your palm just in front of your right ear. Your other hand can help balance the ball (see figure 6.4). Let's try: ready, ball in hand, fingers back."

6. Let students practice this with their own rhythm. Turn the music on and ask them to see if they can get the ball in the right position. Let them practice until the music stops.

7. Now, with the children sitting in their spaces, demonstrate the "puppet." Explain to them that a string is attached from the back of the shooting hand to the same-side knee. So, if the ball is in your shooting hand and you push it up toward the basket the same-side knee will come up also. Demonstrate this puppet phenomenon. Hold the ball the same way a waiter carries a tray of water glasses (see figure 6.5). Ask the children

Figure 6.5   Correct layup position.

to pretend to tie a string from their shooting hand to their same-side knee and push their hand up, then say, "Look, it's a miracle, your knee came up also."

8. Now it is time to put all these movements together (but still without a basket). Ask, "I wonder who can put all these movements together? Dribble on the first step, place the ball on the serving tray on the first quick step, and then do the puppet on the second quick step." Let the students practice pushing the ball upward into the air for a few moments while the music plays. The following is a review for a right-handed person:

- Dribble on the first step with the left foot.
- On the first quick step on the right foot, put the ball in the correct shooting position. The left hand helps balance the ball in the shooting hand.
- On the second quick step, push off with your left foot and extend your right arm and raise your right knee upward.

9. The majority of your students are now ready to push the ball up to the basket and perform a layup. For first, second, and third graders, use a smaller ball and lower the basket to about five or six feet (1.5 or 1.8 m) if you can. If you can't, tape circles on the wall so that the little ones have something to shoot at. Point out that the target will be the square on the backboard. Ask the students where the ball should hit on the square in order to bounce into the basket (it should be the top right-hand corner). After assigning the students to a basket, ask, "Who can make a layup using all the movements we have been practicing?" Start the music and let them practice.

RUNNING SKILLS

I have coached track and cross country for 40 years, so I believe it is important to develop a student's running skills. Track coaches spend a lot of time coaching their athletes in how to run correctly so that they can run faster, but elementary school teachers don't spend much, if any, time on it. We just assume that kids can run correctly, so we play games and carry out activities that encourage running, but we don't often work specifically on improving their skill as runners. I tell my runners and my physical education students that there are only three ways to get faster:

- Increase flexibility
- Increase strength
- Increase running coordination

Stretching exercises are the best way to develop flexibility, and most elementary physical education teachers have access to mats and a stretching program. The activities that follow should help you develop running strength and running coordination in your students.

Building Running Strength

Elementary school students do not attempt strength training like older athletes do, but they can gain specific running strength through the following fun activities. These activities develop both leg and arm strength.

|||||||||||| **Horse and Chariot** ||||||||||||||||||||||||||||||||||||||||||||||||||||||||||||||||||||||||||||||||||||||

GRADES ||||||

K–6

EQUIPMENT ||||||

- Twelve cloth ropes
- Twelve carpet squares
- Music and player, if desired

DESCRIPTION ||||||

The children love this activity, and it gives them a great cardiovascular workout and builds super leg strength.

1. Pair the students and assign one the role of horse and the other the role of chariot driver. Give the horses an 8- to 10-foot-long (2.5-3 m) cloth rope. The middle of the rope goes around the waist of the horse, and the chariot driver, who is lying on a carpet square behind the horse, holds the two ends of the rope (see figure 6.6).
2. When both students are ready, the horse pulls the chariot. The racetrack can be as long as you want—the width of the gym, the length of the gym, or on the road around the gym.
3. Ask each pair, consisting of a horse and a chariot driver, to see how quickly they can complete six lengths of the gym. The pair switches roles after each length of the gym.

Figure 6.6 Horse and Chariot.

Figure 6.7   Make the activity more difficult by adding more resistance to the horse's load.

VARIATIONS ||||||

These variations build leg strength and, at the same time, provide fun.

- To add resistance hook a tire to the feet of the chariot driver (see figure 6.7).
- Add a passenger to the load. The passenger holds onto the ankles of the chariot driver. This creates a tough pull for the horse. The passenger should be lying on a carpet square holding onto the ankles of the chariot driver.

|||||||||||| Mat Push ||||||||||||||||||||||||||||||||||||||||||||||||||||||||||||||||||||||||||||||||||

GRADES ||||||

K–8

EQUIPMENT ||||||

- One folded gym mat for each team of five students
- Three carpet squares per mat
- One stuffed animal per student
- Beanbags (stuffed-animal food)
- Music and player, if desired

DESCRIPTION ||||||

Children love this activity as much as the horse and chariot activity. And you can increase resistance by adding riders on top of the folded mats (see figure 6.8). Everyone will want to

Figure 6.8   Mat Push.

ride. I used this same activity with my senior high sprinters. They pushed pads from the high-jump pit, which are much larger than folded mats, and the coach was the rider.

1. Put one folded mat on top of three carpet squares. Place a stuffed animal on the mat and tell the students that they have to deliver the stuffed animal to its food by pushing the mat to the stuffed-animal food (beanbags at the other end of the gym). Once there they can give the stuffed animal its food and push the mat back to pick up some more food back at the starting line.

2. Here are some variations that add resistance:

- Eliminate the carpet squares from under the mat.
- Separate the students into groups of four. The group will push the mat four lengths of the gym. Each child gets a chance to ride on top of the mat while the other three push. Each child pushes three lengths and rides one.
- Older students can "mat race" from one end of the gym to the other.

Tug-o-War

GRADES

K–8

EQUIPMENT

Tug-o-war rope

DESCRIPTION

Everyone knows how to conduct a tug-o-war contest: Tie a ribbon to the middle of a rope and attempt to pull the ribbon to your team's goal (see figure 6.9). You can try two on two, adding other members during the tug. If one team is close to winning, quickly add another puller to the losing side. Continue until all students are pulling or a team wins. Try five-on-five, six-on-six, or twelve-on-twelve pulls. You don't have to spend a lot of time on tug-o-war to increase the leg strength of your students.

Figure 6.9   Tug-o-War.

IIIIIIIIIIIIII **House Hops** IIIIIIIIIIIIIIIIIIIIIIIIIIIIIIIIIIIIIIIIIIIIIIIIIIIIIIIIIIIIIIIIIIIIIIIIIIIIIIIIIIIIIIIIIIIIIII

GRADES IIIIII

K–8

EQUIPMENT IIIIII

- One cloth jump rope per student
- Mats (optional)

DESCRIPTION IIIIII

This activity uses the principles of plyometrics (increasing muscle power through repeated rapid stretching and contracting of muscles).

1. Tell students to make a square house with their rope, then to stand inside the house (see figure 6.10). Let the children practice forward and backward jumps by leading them through the following questions:

   - Can you jump out the front door into the front yard and then jump backward through the front door back into the house?
   - How quickly can you do it five times?
   - Can you do a 180-degree turn as you jump out and a 180-degree turn as you jump back in?
   - How many of you can jump forward out the front door, jump back in the house backward through the front door, then continue backward out the back door, and then finally forward, back into the house, through the back door? How quickly can you do this? Can you do it again only go through all the doors forward? Backward?

Figure 6.10   House Hops.

2. Now introduce side jumps. Ask the following questions:

- Let's jump out the right side door and then back into the house. Can you do it out the left side door also?
- Go in and out both doors five times. Remember to jump sideways, keeping your body facing the front door.
- I wonder if you can do that again, but during each jump do a 180-degree turn.
- Who can do this series of jumps: front door–house–back door–house–side door–house–other side door–house?

VARIATIONS ||||||

- Try doing the same routine while hopping on one leg, but first make the house much smaller.
- Try the jumping routine while holding a ball or playing catch with a partner. This also builds coordination because the arms now are doing a different activity.
- Try the complete series of jumps—front door, house, back door, house, right side door, house, left side door, house—while jumping rope. Instead of using the rope as a house, pick it up and use it as a jump rope.

|||||||||||| Jumping Rope |||||||||||||||||||||||||||||||||||||||||||||||||||||||||||||||||||

GRADES ||||||

K–8

EQUIPMENT ||||||

One jump rope for each student

DESCRIPTION ||||||

Jumping rope is probably the best way to develop leg strength, and most physical educators are comfortable conducting a jump-rope lesson. Consider giving the students a worksheet with jump-rope tasks pictured on it. When students can complete the rope-jumping trick, they check it off and move to the next trick. Or pair the students, turn the music on, and let them work on jump-rope tricks. Walk around the gym and offer help wherever you can.

The following resources teach jump-rope skills:

A Developmental Jump Rope Task Card Program by Cliff Carnes, 1984, The Education Co., 3949 Linus Way, Carmichael, CA 95608

Skip It for Fun! by Richard Cendali, 1977, Douglas Elementary School, 840 75th Street, Boulder, CO 80303

Aerobic Rope Skipping by Paul Smith, 1981, Educational Activities, Inc., P.O. Box 87, Baldwin, NY 11510

|||||||||||| Horizontal Mountain Climb |||||||||||||||||||||||||||||||||||||||||||||||

GRADES ||||||

K–8

EQUIPMENT ||||||

- One cloth clothesline rope per three students, 50 feet (15 m) or longer depending on the length of your gym (This rope can be purchased at a hardware store in 100-foot [30 m] lengths.)
- One carpet square per three students
- One scooter per three students

Figure 6.11   Horizontal Mountain Climb.

Figure 6.12   Horizontal Mountain Climb while lying on back.

DESCRIPTION //////

1. Group the children in threes—each group should have one rope, one carpet square, and one scooter. Stretch the rope the entire length of the gym. For very young children or for a less strenuous workout, stretch the rope the width of the gym.

2. Two team members, one at each end of the rope, should pull the rope as tight as possible across the floor. The third team member places the scooter over the rope at one end, lies on his or her tummy on the scooter, and grabs the rope with his or her hands (see figure 6.11).

3. The student on the scooter pulls himself or herself hand over hand to the other side of the gym. He or she changes places with the rope holder, who now crosses the gym. Continue this until everyone has a chance to cross the gym.

VARIATIONS //////

- Try pulling across the gym and back—two lengths—before switching.

- Try pulling while the student is lying on the scooter on his or her back. The rope holders will have to hold the rope over the scooter (see figure 6.12).

- Try pulling across while sitting on the scooter.

- Add another partner and another scooter. Have students pull themselves and their partner across. With this variation the students must lie on their tummy with the second student holding onto the puller's ankles (see figure 6.13).

- Try all of these variations using a carpet square rather than a scooter. This variation is pretty tough—your kids probably won't be able to pull a partner across the gym using carpet squares.

Figure 6.13   Horizontal Mountain Climb with a partner.

|||||||||||| **Pull Your Partner to Safety** ||||||||||||||||||||||||||||||||||||||||||||||||||||

GRADES //////

K–8

EQUIPMENT //////

- One cloth clothesline rope per three students, 50 feet (15 m) or longer depending on the length of your gym
- One carpet square per three students

DESCRIPTION //////

1. Group the students in threes. Lay the rope on the floor lengthwise across the gym. Two partners stand at one end of the gym near one end of the rope, and the third partner lies on his or her tummy on a carpet square and holds the other end of the rope (see figure 6.14).
2. When the partner on the carpet square is ready, one partner at the other end pulls hand over hand, while the third partner takes up the slack in the rope so that no one trips over it.

VARIATIONS //////

- Use two pullers and one carpet-square rider.
- Use one puller, one carpet-square rider, and one person riding a scooter and holding the ankles of the person on the carpet square.

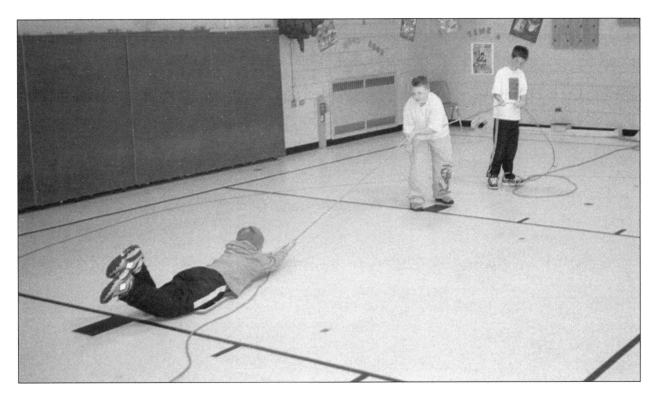

Figure 6.14   Pull Your Partner to Safety.

|||||||||||| Push-Ups |||||||||||||||||||||||||||||||||||||||||||||||||||||||||||||||||||||||||||||||||||||||||

GRADES //////

K–8

EQUIPMENT //////

- One beanbag per group (some exercises group students in pairs, others in threes)
- Scooters (optional)

DESCRIPTION //////

Push-ups are, of course, one of the most common and popular exercises for building arm strength. Students respond well when you challenge them to "make a straight bridge by balancing on their hands and toes" and then try to touch their chin to the floor and push back up. You can give push-up "homework" to first, second, and third graders, recommending that they practice their push-ups during commercial breaks while watching TV. It could get boring after a while if you just practice push-ups. Here are some other activities you can do in the push-up position. These activities are fun and also help develop arm strength.

- **Drop the beanbag.** Two partners face each other in push-up position. A third partner stands between them and drops a beanbag to the floor. The beanbag should land between the two students in push-up position. As soon as the bag hits the floor, each partner attempts to pick it up. Players earn one point for picking up the bag. Rotate positions after each drop. Teachers can decide how many points are needed to win the match.
- **Hand tag.** Partners face each other in push-up position with a line between them. Partner A is "it." While supporting themselves on one arm, partner B attempts to touch the floor over the line to score a point, and partner A tries to tag B as his or her hand crosses the line. As soon as A makes the tag, they change roles.

- **Alternating hand touch.** Partners face each other in push-up position. On a signal, partners try to alternately touch opposite hands (right to right, left to left) as quickly as possible in 30 seconds. Score one point for each touch.
- **Nudge.** Partners, side by side in push-up position facing the same direction, attempt to nudge each other's shoulder and make the other move his or her hand to a new position.
- **Gym scooter activities.** Students perform the road warm-ups presented in chapter 1 (pages 10 to 15), but instead of running the road, they lie facedown on scooters and "drive" the road, propelling themselves with their arms. Students can also pull a partner or a tire while on a scooter—find ways to add resistance. They can try pushing the scooter backward.
- **Gopher River Raft.** This is a neat item. Using the paddles, the rowers work their arms and legs.

Building Running Coordination

The following running-coordination drills greatly enhance running efficiency. Some elementary school PE teachers overlook these drills because they assume their students are naturally skilled enough to run. However, incorporating these fun activities into your classes can help students of all ages become better runners.

Basic Running-Coordination Drills

GRADES

K–12

EQUIPMENT

None needed

DESCRIPTION

Teach these drills in an open space such as a gym, open field, or track. Before executing the drills, remind the kids to use their arms correctly:

- Keep a 90-degree angle at the elbow.
- One hand comes up to the chin, the other hand back to the hip.
- The forefinger and thumb touch lightly; the other fingers curl in and remain relaxed.
- Keep elbows in toward the body.
- Pump the arms in opposition to the legs.

Students line up along a line on the ground and perform these drills for 20 yards (20 m) to another line.

- **Form statue–balance walk.** Take a step. Hold the running position for a fraction of a second, balancing on the ball of one foot and holding the opposite knee high (see figure 6.15).
- **Butt flicks, knees down.** Move toward the line while quickly raising the heels behind and touching them to the butt. The knees point toward the ground (see figure 6.16). Stay on the balls of the feet and use the arms in opposition to the legs.
- **Butt flicks, knees up.** Move toward the other line while raising the feet directly under the body and touching the heels to the butt. Lift the knees high, land on the ball of the foot, and use the arms.

Figure 6.15   Form statue–balance walk.

Figure 6.16   Butt flicks, knees down.

- **Bounce skip.** Using a small skip, lift the knees and swing the arms. Keep the arms in the correct running position.
- **Straight-leg run.** Legs reach and pull, staying straight throughout. Land on the ball of the foot and pull. Remember to use the arms.
- **Broken leg.** Run while one leg remains stiff and the other works normally.
- **Snap run.** On every third step, snap the leg through quickly. You will alternate legs during the drill.

|||||||||||| **Tape Drill** ||||||||||||||||||||||||||||||||||||||||||||||||||||||||||||||||||||||||||||||||

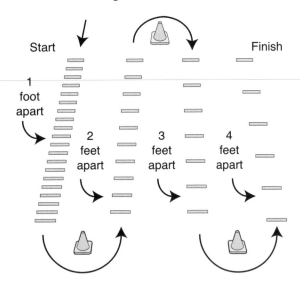

Figure 6.17   Setup for Tape Drill.

GRADES ||||||

1–12

EQUIPMENT ||||||

Three rolls of athletic tape, or chalk

DESCRIPTION ||||||

1. Put four sets of tape marks in a line alongside each other on the track or gym floor, or put chalk marks on the playground. The tape lines should be 20 yards (20 meters) long. The first set contains marks one foot (30 cm) apart, the second set of marks are two feet (60 cm) apart, the third set are three feet (90 cm) apart, and the fourth set are four feet (120 cm) apart.

2. Designate a starting line and finish line, and put cones at the ends of the lines for students to go around (see figure 6.17).

3. Challenge the students to run with high knees and touch each tape mark with their feet. Remind them to swing their arms, lift their knees, and use good running form.

|||||||||||| **Rope Running Drills** |||||||||||||||||||||||||||||||||||||||||||||||||||||||||||||||||||||||||||||

GRADES ||||||

K–8

EQUIPMENT ||||||

One jump rope per student

DESCRIPTION ||||||

These coordination activities are difficult and require a lot of concentration and practice. Students can perform them in the gym or on the playground. If you're doing them in the gym, students can travel the width or the length. If you line up your students along the sideline of the gym, they can all cross the width of the gym at once, and no one has to be concerned about anyone watching them. My students liked these drills because they were challenging, and they often practiced them on the playground during recess. Very young students may be able to do only forward run–forward rope, but keep trying these drills each year.

- **Forward run–forward rope.** The student does a high-knee run across the gym. The rope should pass under each foot as the knee comes up. The student must coordinate twirling the rope with running.

- **Forward run–backward rope.** The student again runs across the gym with high knee lift. Now, however, the knee must stay up slightly longer as the rope passes backward under each foot as the knee comes up.

- **Backward run–forward rope.** This is similar to forward run–forward rope, except that the student runs backward as the rope twirls forward, passing under each foot as the knee comes up.

- **Backward run–backward rope.** This is very difficult. The knee again must stay up slightly longer.

HURDLING

Hurdling is a difficult and advanced skill, one that helps students develop overall body coordination. It is also a fun skill for children to learn. It is important to provide children with hurdles of different heights and allow them to go over the height they feel comfortable with. You will be surprised at how quickly their confidence develops so that they want to attempt a more difficult height. Showing the students pictures of Olympians hurdling will help them understand the concept.

To introduce hurdling technique to your students, ask them the following series of questions:

- What limb goes over the hurdle first? (Answer: your favorite leg.) Let's give this leg a name: College and Olympic hurdlers call it the *lead leg*.
- What's the second body part to go over the hurdle? (Answer: the opposite arm.) Let's call this the *lead arm*.
- What do you think the third limb to go over the hurdle is? (Answer: the other arm). We call this the *trail arm*.
- Who can guess what we call the last limb to go over the hurdle? That's right, the *trail leg*.

Now let's do some drills that will help us practice coordinating all these body parts.

Beginning Hurdling

GRADES

K–8

EQUIPMENT

- Twenty to thirty jump ropes
- Ten 6- to 9-inch hurdles for grades K through 3
- Ten 12- to 18-inch hurdles for grades 4 through 6
- Ten 18- to 24-inch hurdles for middle school (You may want to use higher hurdles depending on the size and skill of your students.)
- Cones (one less than the number of rows of ropes you set up)

DESCRIPTION

With kindergarten and first-grade students, start by laying the ropes on the gym floor about 5 yards (4.5 m) apart. There can be as many as four lines of ropes going the length of the gym (see figure 6.18).

1. Challenge the students to run and leap or "step" over each rope. Like in the tape drill, the students should run around a cone at the end of the line and then run and step over the next line. Challenge the students to take off on one foot and land on the other. Watch for students "jumping" over the ropes (taking off on two feet and landing on two feet).

2. One student should hurdle two ropes before the next person goes. This timing sequence allows half the class to run and hurdle over the ropes with very little standing around.

3. After three or four attempts at hurdling the ropes, put a 6-inch-high hurdle near one end of some ropes. The students can choose to hurdle the rope or the hurdle. If you don't have enough hurdles to place next to every rope, randomly place as many as you have.

4. After several attempts with the 6-inch hurdles, place 12-inch hurdles next to the remaining ropes. Students can now choose between hurdling a rope, a 6-inch hurdle, or a

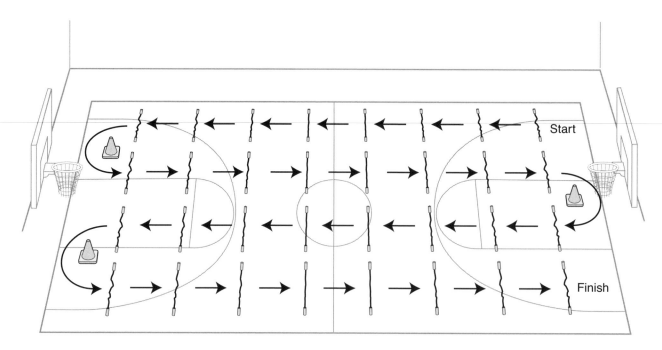

Figure 6.18 Setup for Beginning Hurdling.

12-inch hurdle. This is a heck of a workout, so after the students have gone through the hurdle course several times, set up a row of ropes, a row of 6-inch hurdles, and two rows of 12-inch hurdles. Challenge the students to practice their hurdle skills over the lower heights, and when they have gained confidence and skill, to move on to a higher hurdle.

‖‖‖‖‖‖‖‖‖‖ Hurdling Wall Drills ‖‖

GRADES ‖‖‖‖

1–12

EQUIPMENT ‖‖‖‖

Athletic tape

DESCRIPTION ‖‖‖‖

Practice this series of drills during your track unit before letting students attempt correct hurdle form over the hurdles. When describing correct hurdle technique, tell students to step quickly over the hurdle and snap their lead leg down quickly. Explain to them that flying through the air slows them down. They should try to get back onto the track quickly and sprint to the next hurdle. Tell students to aim the knee at the center of the hurdle and to keep their eyes on the center of the hurdle. The lead foot will come up and clear the hurdle first, and they should try to keep the lead leg slightly bent when clearing the hurdle.

Before conducting the drill, place strips of tape on the wall about 18 to 24 inches (46-60 cm) high. Mark large dots on the strips to serve as targets. Students find a place along the wall, making sure that they have enough room to do the drill without kicking or hitting their neighbor. Students back away from the wall two to four feet (60 cm to 120 cm), depending on their age and size, and face the target.

Figure 6.19 Practice hitting the target with the ball of the foot of the lead leg.

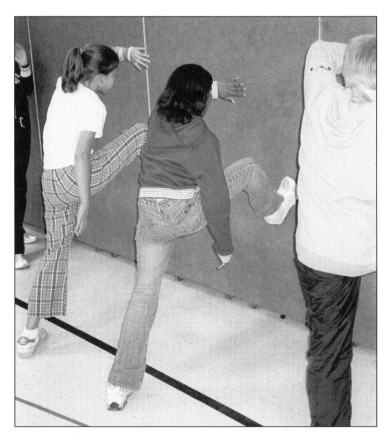

Figure 6.20 The lead arm blocks the sun.

Lead Leg

With students facing their target, explain to these young hurdlers that every time you clap your hands, they are to drive their knee up, extend their leg, and hit the spot with the bottom of their shoe (see figure 6.19). Ask them if they can hit the spot with the ball of their foot. Clap your hands five times, letting the students practice hitting their spot. After the sixth clap yell, "Freeze." Ask them the following questions while their lead foot is on the spot:

- Is your lead knee slightly bent?
- How many can lean forward and put their chest close to the lead-leg thigh?
- Who kept their heel from hitting the spot?

Lead Arm

Remind students that the lead arm is the arm opposite from their lead leg. The position for the lead arm is elbow up and palm out, or "blocking the sun." Explain to the students that now when you clap your hands, their lead foot will hit the spot, their knee will be slightly bent, and the lead arm will block the sun (see figure 6.20). Clap five times, then on the sixth repetition yell, "Freeze" and ask the following questions:

- Is the ball of your foot close to your wall spot?
- Is your lead knee bent?
- Are you leaning forward with your chest close to your lead-leg thigh?
- Is your lead-arm elbow up slightly higher than your head?
- Is your lead-arm palm facing out, blocking the sun?
- Can you look at the wall under your lead-arm wrist?

Trail Arm

If your right leg is your lead leg and your left arm is your lead arm, then your right arm is the trail arm. The rule for the trail arm is "Let's go out for dinner—you are buying. Reach for your wallet." Explain that when you are going over the hurdle

Figure 6.21 Practicing trail-leg position.

the left arm (lead arm) is blocking the sun and the right arm (trail arm) is about 6 to 12 inches (15 to 30 cm) away from your right hip, ready to reach for your wallet. Let students practice five times against the wall. This time when you yell freeze on the sixth repetition, ask if their trail arm is in the correct position.

Trail Leg

For our right-footed lead-leg hurdler, the left leg is the trail leg. The rule for the trail leg is *knee under armpit.* We will now use the wall in a slightly different manner. The children should stand about three feet (1 m) away from the wall, lean forward without moving their feet, and place the palms of their hands on the wall. Now give them the following directions:

- Turn your left (trail leg) toe out.
- Raise your left (trail leg) knee and bring it as high as you can—try to move it in close to your left armpit (see figure 6.21).

- Now step forward quickly on your left foot and at the same time bring your left arm back.

It is now time to allow the students to pick the hurdle height they feel most comfortable with and practice the wall-drill skills over the hurdle. You will think you are an Olympic track coach when your students start going over the hurdles with good form.

THROWING AND CATCHING SKILLS

There are many sports, games, and activities that give students the opportunity to throw and catch. It's best to teach the skills first and then give students the opportunity to practice them in sport and game contexts. Teaching the proper way to throw should be presented as early as first grade.

Learning to catch is quite a developmental process. And there are products on the market now that can help kids learn how to catch. However, these are the products I used in the developmental process. You may choose other objects, but remember to start with slow-moving large objects and progress to faster smaller ones. When we want to develop the skill of throwing and catching it is important that we start with something that moves slowly enough that a very young child can achieve success. The following list of equipment is arranged from slowest to fastest. Introducing the equipment in this developmental sequence gradually challenges students.

- Bubbles
- Scarf or plastic grocery bag
- Balloon
- Balloon inside a balloon
- Balloon inside a balloon, with tape around the balloon (see figure 6.22)

Figure 6.22 Balloon inside a balloon, with tape around the balloon.

- Beach ball (start large, then use progressively smaller balls)
- Volleyball trainer or playground ball
- Foam ball, 5 to 6 inches (13 to 15 cm) in diameter
- Ring, beanbag, fleece ball
- Tennis ball

This sequence may be slightly different from what you use. The important thing is to choose equipment that moves at a speed appropriate for the student's developmental level and to gradually introduce equipment that is more difficult to catch.

Ribbons

GRADES

K–3

EQUIPMENT

One ribbon on a stick per student

DESCRIPTION

The objective of this lesson is to isolate the throwing arm and give children practice in controlling that arm. Each child has a ribbon stick; therefore, they should be spread out throughout the gym so that they can practice these skills without hitting each other. Ask the children the following problem-solving questions:

- Who can make big circles with their ribbons using their favorite hand?
- Who can make big circles forward?
- Can you practice backward circles?
- Can you make big circles with your other hand? Forward? Backward?
- Can you put the ribbon stick in your favorite hand and make a snake on the floor? Can you keep the snake moving?
- Who can make a snake with the other hand?
- I wonder if we can make small circles with the ribbon stick?
- Can you make small circles with the other hand?
- Who can make the ribbon go around their body by passing it from hand to hand?
- Oh-oh, the lion has gotten out of the cage. Can you whip him back into the cage? (Demonstrate an overhand "whip" with the ribbon stick.)
- Can you whip the lion with the other hand? (This movement will be a preliminary overhand throw.)

Use your imagination and let the students get more practice with the ribbon stick.

|||||||||||||| **Poly Spot Throwing** ||||||||||||||||||||||||||||||||||||||||||||||||||||||||||||

GRADES ||||||

K–3

EQUIPMENT ||||||

- Two poly spots per student
- Five tennis balls or beanbags per student
- Two targets such as pins or plastic milk bottles for each student

DESCRIPTION ||||||

In this exercise, students will throw a tennis ball at a target. You can put the targets—pins, plastic jugs, upside-down cones, and so on—on tables or on the floor or hang them from the volleyball standards. Be creative, kids will be more motivated to throw if they have a target that is fun to throw at. Note: Students should first do this drill using an underhand roll with the targets on the floor before trying it with an overhand throw. Also, ask your district tennis coach or your local racket club for old tennis balls they would otherwise throw away; they are great for throwing practice.

1. Place two poly spots for each child along the midline of the gym, one spot behind the other. Tell the students to get five tennis balls out of the box and then stand on the poly spot closest to the targets, which are set up along the sideline of the gym (see figure 6.23). Move the targets closer for younger students. The students can keep one ball in their hand and place the other four behind them.

2. Say to the students, "I wonder if you can knock down those targets by throwing overhand? When I say start, throw one ball at a time and try to hit as many targets as you can. When all of your tennis balls are gone, just wait on your poly spot until I tell you to pick up five tennis balls." When everyone has thrown all their tennis balls, ask them to run and pick up five balls and hustle back to their base.

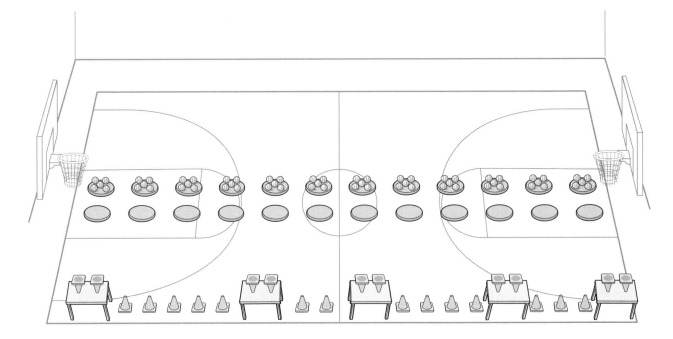

Figure 6.23 Setup for Poly Spot Throwing.

3. Next tell the students, "Now put the balls on the floor behind you, and put your other poly spot in front of you, about one shoe length in front of the first spot and slightly to the left. Put your right foot on the spot you stood on before, and put your left foot on the other spot." A left-handed person would do the opposite. Because this book gives directions only for right-handed students, remember to cue the left-handers when giving directions. Demonstrate a throw with the feet in the correct position. After the demonstration ask the students, "Can you knock down a target with one foot on each base?" Let them try overhand throws.

4. After everyone has thrown again say, "Run and pick up five balls and set up the targets you knocked over." Then say, "Now let's put both feet on the back base, the base your right foot was on. Do you think you can step to the base in front of you with your left foot as you throw? Remember, step with your left foot." Demonstrate the step and throw. Let students practice throwing five balls at the targets using this technique. When they're done, instruct them to run and pick up five balls and set up the targets they knocked over.

5. Now say, "I wonder if you can do this very difficult trick. Stand on the back base and hold the ball in front of you with your palm up and point the ball toward the target you want to hit. Now swing the ball down, and then reach back and then step forward to the front base as you throw the ball. This is called a windup. It is for overhand throwing. The palm will rotate to the natural position as you swing it back. Say the sequence with me as I do it: Swing down—reach back—step and throw." Repeat the demonstration of the sequence while students say the steps, then let them practice the sequence themselves by throwing at the targets five times. Before they begin practice, remind them to hold the ball out at arm's length aiming at the target. While they practice, walk around and help the students who are having difficulty.

6. Say, "Now I want you to move the base that was in front of your left foot. Put it directly in front of your other base—about one shoe length. Now, stand on the back base, but turn sideways. Your left shoulder will point at the targets. Your body should not face the targets anymore, but the end wall. Left-handed students face the other wall. Let's practice without a ball. We will practice the swing down, reach back, and step and throw while we are facing sideways. Can you do it? Practice five times without a ball. Face the end wall. Aim the ball at the target. Swing down, reach back, and step to the front base as you throw." Let the kids practice this sequence five times without a ball.

7. Say, "Okay, super. Now we will learn the most difficult throwing skill. I hope you can do it. I have been practicing and practicing, and I think I finally have it. Watch. I am going to face the targets. When I do my windup, my arm swings back, and when it does, it turns my body sideways to face the end wall. I do a pivot on my right foot, and then I step to the front base with my left foot, and throw. So now our sequence will be (facing the target) swing down, reach back and turn, then step and throw. Wow! This is getting difficult. Who thinks they can do it? Okay, throw five." Continue practicing this last rhythmical sequence. You can also let everyone throw at once as you shout the sequential steps. Encourage them to whisper the steps as they throw.

|||||||||||||| **Tossing and Catching Challenges** |||||||||||||||||||||||||||||||||||||||

GRADES ||||||

K–6

EQUIPMENT ||||||

Age-appropriate equipment for tossing and catching (see list on pages 106-107)

DESCRIPTION ||||||

Give each child a ball or other age-appropriate item to toss and catch. The students do not all have to use the same type of equipment; you can use whatever items you have on hand that are age appropriate. Ask the students to spread out, finding their own space. Ask the children the following questions to give them as many catching experiences as possible.

- Can you practice tossing the ball up and catching it in your own space? Don't toss it so high that you miss it.
- Can you toss and catch while walking in the big space? How many can do this without touching their friends? Can you run, skip, hop, gallop, slide, leap, and so on while throwing and catching? Remember, no collisions.
- Can you walk backward while tossing and catching? Be very careful about collisions.
- Who can walk sideways and throw and catch? Skip? Hop? Run? Gallop? Slide? Jump?
- Can you quickly change your direction every time you hear my signal?
- Who can change ways to move every time you hear my signal?
- Can you walk as tall or as high as you can while you are throwing and catching?
- Can you walk as low as possible while throwing and catching?
- Who can gradually change levels while throwing and catching? Is it difficult to do this?
- Try to go very slowly from high to low while you are catching. Who can do it?
- Can you quickly go from low to high while walking and catching? Do this many times. Try it skipping and jumping.
- Who can find a new way to throw and catch while at a low level? High level?
- Let's work with speed now and see who can catch the ball. Who can run fast and throw and catch at the same time? Now try to run in slow motion and catch.
- Who can gradually change speeds while throwing and catching?
- Who in this class can walk heavy as a rock while throwing and catching?
- Can you make your whole body stiff and strong and then walk or run while throwing and catching?
- Try to be as loose as a rubber band. Now can you walk, throw, and catch?
- Can you float like a feather while throwing and catching? Be as light as you can.

VARIATIONS ||||||

- Add new locomotor movements.
- Put the children with a partner and instruct the pair to toss and catch.
- Add other types of equipment to throw and catch such as beanbags, balloons, etc.
- Ask, "Who can find new and different ways to handle the ball?"
- Make up new problems combining the ones already used. The following are examples:
  - Can you walk backward quickly while catching?
  - Who can skip sideways at a high level while throwing and catching?

- On my signal, change level and direction. Let's see who can do it without missing the ball.
- Change level and speed.
- Change direction and speed.
- Change force and speed. Float slowly and then quickly.
- Who can change their direction and speed while throwing and catching at a high level?
- Let's run in slow motion at a medium level. Change directions on the signal. Now move quickly at a low level. Did anyone drop the ball?
- Skip lightly and slowly while throwing and catching. Change to a fast, strong, straight walk on my signal.

Try all the locomotor movements with the earlier examples. Ask the students to perform the movements while varying speed, direction, force, and level. Have the children think of new ways to combine movements while they are throwing and catching the ball or other items.

The children can work with partners or in small groups on all of the problems they worked on individually. Here are some sample problems for partners:

- How quickly can you and your partner toss the ball back and forth to each other?
- Can you and your partner move and change directions many times while throwing and catching?
- Can you change levels while throwing and catching with your partner?

All of the commands listed previously can be used with different types of equipment. If you are starting a football unit, use footballs. In the spring, start your softball unit with these commands and problem-solving questions.

To help children learn ball-handling skills, ask this question: Who can find new and different ways to use the ball?" I've listed some of the answers my students have given.

- Throw the ball up with the feet and catch it with the hands.
- Throw the ball up, turn in a circle, and catch it.
- Throw the ball up, bounce it on the head, and catch it.
- Gradually go from tiptoes to lying down while throwing and catching the ball.
- Throw the ball up and clap the hands as many times as possible before catching.

POLKA STEP

Our last sport skill is the polka step. This step requires a quick transfer of weight and is very difficult for young children to learn. To learn the polka step correctly, students must first learn how to gallop.

|||||||||||| Polka Step Progression ||||||||||||||||||||||||||||||||||||||||||||||||||||||||

GRADES //////

K–3

EQUIPMENT //////

Music and player (optional)

DESCRIPTION //////

1. While the students are sitting in their own space, demonstrate the gallop and say, "I am going to put my favorite foot forward and gallop. Watch. Now, did you notice that my favorite foot was very selfish? It never let my other foot go first. My favorite foot always stayed in front. I wonder if you can do this. Stand up. When I start the music, gallop around the gym and put your selfish favorite foot first. Never let your other foot go in front. Ready? Go." Let the students practice this gallop for three to four minutes or the length of a song. Then go through the same routine with the other foot in front. The favorite foot now has to follow.

2. Say, "Wow, that was great. Now I have a difficult challenge for you. Who thinks they can gallop with their favorite foot forward, but when I clap my hands, the other foot becomes the leader? Who thinks they can do it without stopping? Okay, let's try." Put the music on again. After 15 to 20 seconds, signal that they should change the lead foot.

3. Say, "Now without music playing, we will gallop eight times with the favorite foot forward and then switch and gallop eight times with the other foot leading. I will count it out. Good luck. I don't know if you will be able to do this. It is very difficult. Ready? Go." Don't pause when the students switch feet; keep them galloping smoothly from one foot to the next.

4. Say, "Very good. Now let's try this again, but we will do six gallops and then switch and let the other foot lead for six." Repeat this process for four gallops, then two gallops, then switch the lead foot after every gallop. The students will do a small skip as they change lead feet. Now challenge them to slow it down while they change lead feet. Ask them to walk the gallop forward a few times.

5. Next, challenge them to gallop sideways. "I know you can change feet doing the gallop walk forward, but I wonder if you can do it side to side. Watch me." Demonstrate and count out one-two-three and one-two-three while going side to side. Say, "Okay, here we go! Everyone to my count." Let the kids practice.

6. Your students are now doing the basic polka step. Gradually count the tempo faster and instruct the kids to stay on the balls of their feet. Your classes will have a lifetime of polka-dancing fun at wedding dances.

This chapter provided key words and a progression for teaching sport skills. These exercises are fun to teach, and kids love to learn them. Ask local college or high school athletes to come in and demonstrate some of these skills. Let the kids compose a letter to one of their local heroes asking if they would come to class and show them how to do a layup, or go over a hurdle. Using problem-solving questions and letting kids have plenty of practice time by themselves or with a partner are keys in learning sport skills.

Part III

Putting It All Together

Part III features activities that combine skills and proficiencies from many areas of the physical education curriculum. Chapter 7 offers obstacle courses and station activities, staples of PE fun. Kids love obstacle courses because they provide a new challenge, and teachers love them because they build students' fitness and coordination. Station activities are a great way to teach or review curriculum.

Now that we are discovering so much about how movement and thinking are connected, PE teachers are seeking activities that build this brain–body connection. Chapter 8 has activities that integrate academic subject areas in a fitness-building context, letting your students practice their moving and thinking at the same time.

In chapter 9 I present skill-building games I have been using for years, probably before some of you were born. These games offer fun, competition, and maximum participation and movement opportunities. I hope your students enjoy them as much as mine have.

Chapter 7

Obstacle Courses and Station Activities

O bstacle courses and stations offer a variety of learning environments limited only by your imagination. Obstacle courses provide a fun and challenging way for students to gain motor skills. Station activities provide a quick and effective way for students to review and practice their skills. This chapter presents unique and challenging obstacle courses and station activities.

OBSTACLE COURSES

Obstacle courses offer the following benefits:

- **Motor planning.** Kids must plan a route or a movement or use a series of movements to move around, over, under, and through obstacles.
- **Strength.** Include strength building in your courses. The students may have to crawl, climb, or support their weight on their hands in order to complete the course.
- **Endurance.** When the students are familiar with the course, time them. It is exhausting to attempt to set a new time record over a tough obstacle course.
- **Agility.** This is the ability to move our bodies in different directions quickly and efficiently. These obstacle courses force students to change direction with their bodies or with parts of their bodies many different times.
- **Fun.** You can design any type of obstacle course, and no matter what you design, students will eagerly accept the challenge.

When setting up a course, remember to keep safety in mind. Provide plenty of mats if the students will jump off anything. Playing music while the students make their way through the obstacle course adds a sense of fun to the activity. Depending on the setup, students can try the course five or six times before the end of the period. Monitor how many times each student gets to try the course. Sometimes, this is so much fun that the more athletic students push past their more reserved classmates. If students must wait before trying the course, remind them to be polite and allow everyone to have a chance.

############## **Electric Fence** ##

1–12

- One roll of baling twine (5,000 feet [1,524 m], preferably bright orange)
- Thirty rip flags
- Twenty hoops
- Ten tires
- Ten cones
- Twenty anchors such as gym standards, tables, folded mats, and so on
- Stopwatch (optional)

My earliest obstacle course was challenging to build as well as challenging for the students to complete. I set up this course at Jefferson Elementary in Winona, Minnesota, in 1968.

1. Place gym standards, tables, tires, bleachers, or anything heavy that can serve as twine anchors along each sideline of the gym. String the twine back and forth across the width of the gym all the way down to the opposite free throw line, circling the anchors at different heights (see figure 7.1). Use as many gym volleyball standards as you can find. Your course will be different depending on the materials you have available. One roll of baling twine is plenty if your gym is about 60 feet (18 m) wide. The highest strand of twine should be about as high as your tallest student and the lowest should be just below knee height to allow students to crawl under it. Students will crawl over, climb through, and duck under the twine as they make their trip from one end of the gym to the other.

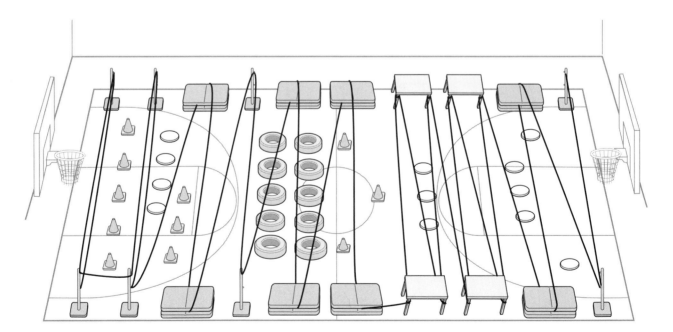

Figure 7.1   Setup for Electric Fence.

2. Now paper clip the rip flags to the twine. Disperse them as equally as you can throughout the gym. Tell the students that the flags are electric, and no one should touch them.

3. Spread out the hoops throughout the roped area. Tell the students that they may not touch them because they are sink holes and no one wants to get caught in a sink hole.

4. Place the cones throughout the course. The students do not want to touch the cones either because they are volcanoes that could erupt when touched.

5. Distribute the tires throughout the course. The tires are safe spots where students can sit and rest during their journey.

6. When the students enter the gym, put them in teams of five at one open end of the gym. Tell them that they must travel to the other end of the gym without touching the twine, rip flags, hoops, or cones. Once they make it to the other end they must return to the original starting line, but they must choose a different path back. Allow the students to make as many trips as they can during the class period. Students will enjoy this course—you can make it easier or more difficult, depending upon the ages and skill of your students.

VARIATIONS //////

- Time students.
- Go through while connected to a partner.
- Let teams start at opposite ends and do not allow them to touch each other as they pass by each other in the middle. The teams will have to cooperate as they pass on the course. They cannot touch, so someone may have to let someone else go first.

Jungle Trail

GRADES //////

K–12

EQUIPMENT //////

- Two benches
- Two tables
- Twenty cones
- One wooden ladder
- One low balance beam or a 10-foot-long (3 m) 2-by-6 (5 × 15 cm)
- One 10-foot-long (3 m) 2-by-4 (5 × 10 cm)
- Six basketballs
- Six rings
- One basketball hoop
- Twelve jump ropes
- Two low hurdles
- Two high hurdles
- Stopwatch (optional)

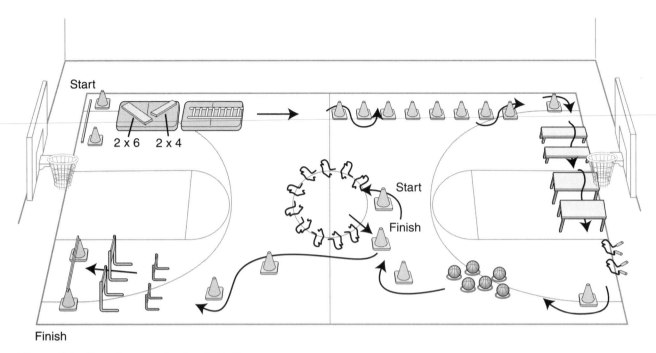

Figure 7.2   Sample setup for Jungle Trail.

DESCRIPTION ///////

Use equipment to set up an imaginative and challenging obstacle course (see figure 7.2). The following describes the course I have set up.

1. The students start by walking across the boards on the mat, then traverse the ladder's rungs (stepping on them rather than between them).
2. Students weave in and out of the cones.
3. Students must go around the outside of the two corner-marking cones.
4. Students go over the first bench and under the second bench and then over the first table and under the second. Make sure the bench is stable when the student goes over.
5. Students jump rope 10 times, jumping over the 10 lines around the center circle.
6. Six basketballs are each sitting on the free throw line. The student must make a layup with one ball, return it to its ring and then pick up another ball and dribble 20 times with that ball. After returning the second ball to its ring, the student picks up the third ball and passes it around his or her waist 10 times and returns the third ball to its ring.
7. The students run with high knees over the 10 cloth ropes lying around the center circle.
8. Students jump over the short hurdle and crawl through the higher hurdle and then run to the finish line.

Students can work with a partner and time one another, or they can complete the course without being timed. Start the next student when the previous student has finished weaving through the cones. Set up two sets of hurdles at the end of the course in case students catch the person in front of them. There should not be much waiting around on this obstacle course. Kids are either timing, running the course, or recovering. Time students if they want to be timed, and encourage them to try to improve each time they attempt the course.

VARIATION ///////

Set up two obstacle courses next to each other and allow students to race.

IIIIIIIIIIIII **Overhead Projector Obstacle Course** IIIIIIIIIIIIIIIIIIIIIIIIIIIIIIIIIIIIIII

GRADES IIIIII

1–8

EQUIPMENT IIIIII

Three or four overhead projectors

DESCRIPTION IIIIII

1. Arrange the overhead projectors so that an entire wall is lit up and students will cast a shadow on the wall when they traverse the obstacle course.
2. Arrange dimes or draw dots on the glass plate of the projector so that they cast shadows on the wall at different heights that the students must jump over, duck under, jump and touch, or crawl under (see figure 7.3).
3. Let the students go one at a time the entire length of the wall, maneuvering through the obstacle course. Five or six students could attempt the course at once, if they're spaced evenly.

VARIATIONS IIIIII

- Try the obstacle course while dribbling a ball.
- Try the obstacle course while connected to a teammate.
- Try going through the obstacle course as a team of six holding hands.

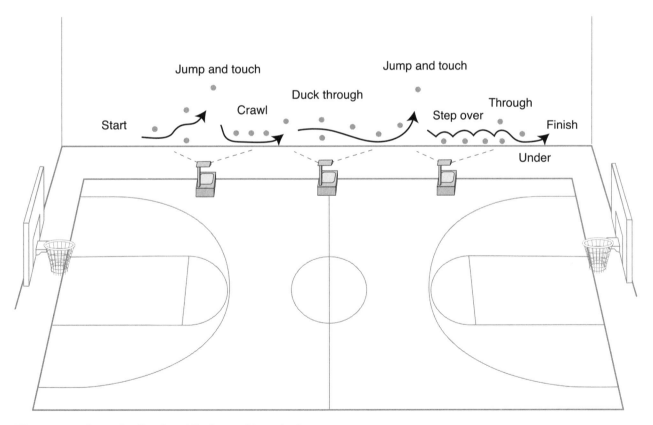

Figure 7.3   Setup for Overhead Projector Obstacle Course.

Activity and diagram adapted, by permission, from D.R. Glover and L.A. Anderson, 2003, *Character education: 43 fitness activities for community building* (Champaign, IL: Human Kinetics), 85-86.

IIIIIIIIIIIIIII **Obstacle Course Homework** IIIIIIIIIIIIIIIIIIIIIIIIIIIIIIIIIIIIIIIIIIIIIIIIIIIIIIIIII

GRADES ///////

K–6

EQUIPMENT ///////

See description

DESCRIPTION ///////

In 1968 I sent a letter home to parents telling them that we had just finished doing obstacle courses in physical education. I encouraged them to build an obstacle course in the backyard during the summer. Parents need to know that they have all the materials they need to build a great obstacle course; they just need to look in the garage or basement for these materials or head out to the local hardware store for a few things.

- Two or three 8-foot-long (2.4 m) boards, two-by-six inches (5 × 15 cm) or two-by-four inches (5 × 10 cm)
- Three 3-foot-long (1 m) dowels, half inch (1.25 cm) in circumference
- Six old paint cans
- Four cardboard boxes
- Eight plastic milk containers
- Three tennis balls
- One basketball
- Six cloth ropes, three feet (1 m) long
- One chair
- Two carpet squares

Figure 7.4 illustrates one way to set up this equipment. But you can also use your imagination to come up with other options.

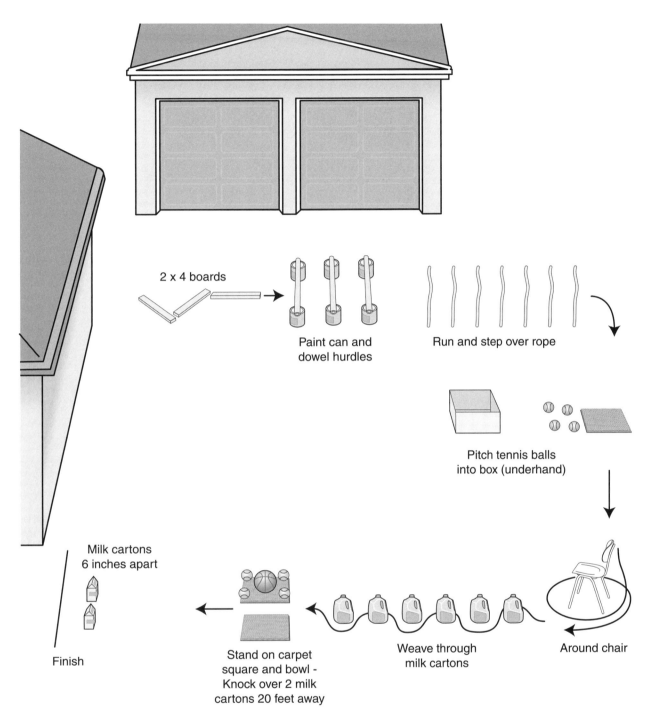

2 x 4 boards

Paint can and dowel hurdles

Run and step over rope

Pitch tennis balls into box (underhand)

Around chair

Weave through milk cartons

Stand on carpet square and bowl - Knock over 2 milk cartons 20 feet away

Milk cartons 6 inches apart

Finish

Figure 7.4 Sample setup for Obstacle Course Homework.

############# **Puzzler** ###

GRADES //////

K–12

EQUIPMENT //////

- One set of Olympet rings (flat agility rings)
- Ten hula hoops
- Six gym tires
- Ten poly spots
- Stopwatch (optional)

DESCRIPTION //////

1. This obstacle course was originally a team-building exercise. Assign each piece of equipment a different body part or combination of body parts to support. The following list provides examples:

   - The blue Olympet ring can only support one foot.
   - The yellow Olympet ring can only support one hand.
   - The red Olympet ring can only support two hands.
   - The white Olympet ring can only support one hand and one foot.
   - The hula hoops can support one or two people but can hold weight for only one minute.
   - The tires are safe places—students can rest on a tire and take their time before planning the rest of their journey.
   - The poly spots are dangerous. They cannot hold weight, and if a student touches one, he or she must go back to the start and begin again.

2. Designate a starting line 6 to 10 feet (1.8 to 3 m) long at one end of the gym. Designate a finish line of the same length at the other end of the gym. Scatter the equipment throughout the space between the start and finish line (see figure 7.5).

3. Students must plan how to get from one end of the gym to the other without breaking the equipment rules. In addition to choosing their path, they will have to plan how to place their bodies in order to get from one piece of equipment to the next.

4. You will have to carefully plan several different routes and place the equipment so that students can actually make it from one end of the course to the other. They may have to stretch and strain and balance themselves in different positions, but they should be able to make it. For example, it would not be possible to cross the gym if you placed too many poly spots together without providing some kind of body-support ring. Once you set up the course, you can leave it up all day, making only minor adjustments in distance for different age levels.

5. The students can take as much time as they need to get from one end of the puzzler to the other.

VARIATIONS //////

- Ask students to try going through the course connected to a partner.
- Put the students in groups of six to eight and let them build their own courses.
- Time the students and establish a class record.
- Show the students the equipment rules once and challenge them to remember the rule for each piece of equipment.

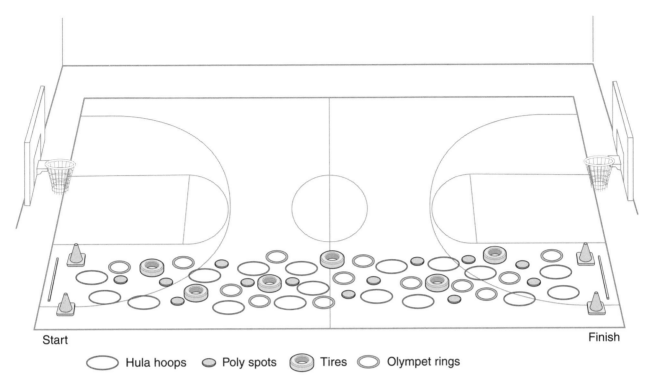

Start   Finish

⬭ Hula hoops   ◉ Poly spots   ◎ Tires   ◯ Olympet rings

Figure 7.5   Setup for Puzzler.

‖‖‖‖‖‖‖‖‖ Agility Obstacle Course ‖‖‖

GRADES ‖‖‖‖

K–12

EQUIPMENT ‖‖‖‖

- Sidewalk chalk or agility mats from a retailer that sells PE equipment such as Gopher Sport
- Stopwatch (optional)

DESCRIPTION ‖‖‖‖

Children love to draw designs and pictures with sidewalk chalk. They also use the chalk to draw hopscotch and foursquare courts (at least they did in the '70s). I have used the chalk to draw agility patterns on our outdoor blacktop playground.

Using this key, red dots for the right foot, blue dots for the left foot, and white squares for both feet together, draw on the blacktop a series of progressively more difficult patterns for the feet to follow. Each pattern should require agility, balance, and quick thinking from the students. Draw five patterns in fairly close proximity to one another and instruct the students to try each pattern at least four times. You can also give the chalk to groups of students and ask them to draw their own agility pattern. Then let each group try the other groups' creations.

When you draw your patterns don't worry about making them perfectly symmetrical. The students will have to adjust their movements to the pattern, so it doesn't matter if it is not uniform. Figure 7.6 illustrates a sample setup.

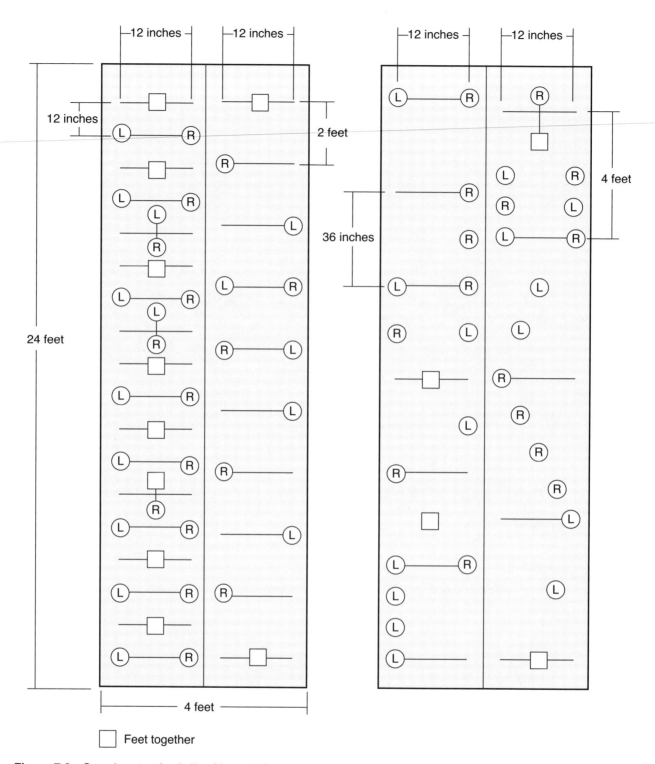

Feet together

Figure 7.6 Sample setup for Agility Obstacle Course.
Reprinted by permission from Gopher Sport.

VARIATIONS ///////

- Time the students on each of the patterns.
- Let them try a pattern while holding an object, such as a large beach ball.
- Using a product such as the Gopher Sport Developmental Agility Mat will save you a lot of drawing time.

STATION ACTIVITIES

Stations are a great way to practice and improve skills. You can set up stations to practice skills that you have been working on in a particular unit, or you can set up stations to improve strength, balance, and eye–hand coordination.

You can set up stations in the morning and leave them up all day, making minor adjustments for the age and skill level of your students. Use music to signal students to move to the next station. Students can practice at each station while the music is playing, and when the music stops, the students can move to the next station. Give students progress check cards to mark their achievement, and allow one student to try as many repetitions as possible at a station while his or her partner counts the successes and marks the card. Students then switch roles for another round at that station. Following are a couple of my favorite station activities.

Eye–Hand Coordination Stations

GRADES

K–8

EQUIPMENT

The amount of equipment you will need depends on the size of your class. The equipment list is just a guideline. You may have other items to throw or catch.

- Frisbees
- Fleece or yarn balls (These can be purchased from Gopher Sport catalog.)
- Stacking cups
- Basketballs and basket
- Four scoops and two scoop balls
- Various targets (see description)
- Stopwatches

DESCRIPTION

Set up five stations around the outside of the gym or put one station in each of the four corners and one station in the center of the gym.

Station 1: Frisbees

Partners attempt to throw and catch the Frisbee as many times in succession as they can without a miss. They can also throw the Frisbee at a target on the wall or a Frisbee golf target.

Station 2: Yarn Balls

Partners attempt to set records throwing and catching yarn balls. You can also provide interesting targets for the students, such as pins set up on tables. Or have students try to hit a basketball and move it to a certain spot. Draw a Halloween goblin target on a big piece of white paper, or let the students draw their own targets and tape them to the wall.

Station 3: Cup Stack

Allow the students to try to set records stacking and unstacking the cups. Provide a couple of stopwatches and let partners time each other.

Station 4: Basketballs and Basket

Challenge the students to shoot baskets from different spots on the floor, keeping track of how many they make and how many they attempt.

Station 5: Scoops

These are difficult items for many students to handle. Challenge students to see how high they can throw the ball and still catch it. Students could keep track of how many times they can successfully throw and catch with a partner using a scoop.

Balance Stations

GRADES

K–6

EQUIPMENT

- Six to eight folding gym mats
- Ten poly spots
- One to three ladders
- Five 8-foot-long (2.5 m) boards, 2-by-4 (5 × 10 cm) and 2-by-6 (5 × 15 cm)
- T-stools or Stabili-T-Stools
- Balance boards
- Stopwatch

DESCRIPTION

Set up five stations around the outside of the gym or put one station in each of the four corners and one station in the center of the gym.

Station 1: Poly Spot Stepping Stones

It is fun to give the stations creative names. For example, call the poly spots "lily pads" and ask the students to step on the lily pads to cross the swamp. Set up this station so that students must cross over the midline at least twice during the trip through the lily pads. You can also set out poly spots in two colors and tell students one color is for one foot and one color is for the other. Students should try to cross the swamp as many times as they can before the music stops. To make this station more difficult use Gopher Sport River Stones. These "stones" are plastic domes that are difficult to walk and balance on.

Station 2: Ladders

Set up one, two, or three ladders, depending upon how many you can find. You can lay them on the ground on mats in a straight line or at angles. Students must walk on the rungs, walk on the side rails, or walk between the rungs without touching them. Ask students to carry a ball while trying to walk across the ladder.

Station 3: Bridges

Set out several wide boards—8-foot-long (2.5 m) 2-by-6s (5 × 15 cm) and 2-by-4s (5 × 10 cm)—on mats as shown in figure 7.7. Your custodian may have some in his or her storage area. These boards serve as bridges that span a deep cavern. Ask students to cross the bridge as many times as they can. You can also ask students carry a ball across the bridge or play catch with a partner as they cross.

Station 4: T-Stool or Stabili-T-Stool

I have used wooden T-stools, but the retailer Sportime carries a product called the Stabili-T-Stool. This tube forces students to balance themselves while performing activities from a seated position. They can be used as cones, target pins, or obstacles to run through and around.

The following are challenges you can give students using a T-stool or Stabili-T-Stool:

- Sit on your tube or stool and try to keep your body as still as possible for 10 seconds.
- Reach forward with your right leg and left arm, and try to hold this position for 10 seconds.
- Reach forward with your left leg and right arm, and try to hold this position for 10 seconds.

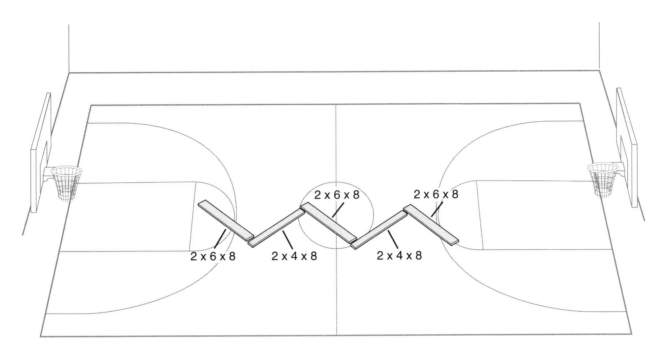

Figure 7.7   Setup for Bridges balance station.

- Let's try to alternate. Every time I clap, you extend your right leg and left arm forward, then left leg and right arm forward.
- Can you march your feet while sitting? How high can you lift your knees?
- Try touching the floor with your hands in front of you.
- Touch the floor on your right side with your right hand and then try to touch the floor on your left side with your left hand.
- Try turning in a circle while sitting on the tube or stool.
- Play catch while sitting on the tube or stool.
- Can you kick a foam ball back and forth with a partner?

Station 5: Balance Boards or Balance Discs

Challenge students to balance in a stationary position for 10 seconds. Today, retailers such as Gopher Sport offer many different types of balance boards. I wish they had been available to me years ago.

Students can try various tasks while using any type of balance board. The following are examples of tasks:

- Throwing at a target
- Catching a beanbag
- Touching the floor and standing back up

Using the balance boards could present a few safety concerns, so always use this equipment on a mat.

Chapter 8

Interdisciplinary Activities

Many students learn better when they are active, so physical education can greatly support the academic classroom by presenting math, spelling, geography, and other subjects through activity. Almost any concept that is presented in the academic classroom can be reinforced in the gym. Many physical education teachers are adding and looking for more interdisciplinary activity ideas as their districts emphasize them more and more. Sporting goods companies now recognize this fact and promote many interdisciplinary ideas within their product selections. This chapter presents activities to reinforce math, spelling, character education, and team building that also help keep children fit.

Scramble Scrabble

GRADES

K–8

EQUIPMENT

One Scramble game

DESCRIPTION

I found this activity in the Gopher Sport catalog. It is not as physically strenuous as Flag Frenzy (see page 130), but it teaches students to cooperate and work together while creating a word.

1. Randomly scatter the 98 Scramble game tiles facedown along one end of the gym.
2. Divide the class into four equal teams and assign each team a name or number. Station the teams at the opposite end of the gym from the Scramble tiles.
3. Designate locomotor movements for the teams to use when retrieving tiles; for example, the first set of retrievers must run. The next retrievers in line must skip, the next must hop, and so on. To make the game more physically challenging, load the path between the teams and the Scramble tiles with obstacles.
4. Start the game by signaling the first person from each team to race to the tile area and retrieve one tile. Then he or she races back to the team and tags the next person in line.
5. When every person on a team has retrieved a tile, they sit down at the start line and begin to assemble a word.
6. After a team has finished retrieving tiles they begin to create as many words as they can with their letters. All teams then rotate turns in a clockwise manner. All words from the other teams will build off of team one's beginning words. The words stay intact, like

words on a Scrabble board. If team one is unable to create a word, then team two begins. Continue the puzzle building in rounds until no more words can be created with the four teams' letters. Teams with extra Scramble tiles at the end of the round retain them in their team area and can use them in the next round.

7. After the first round is completed, start round two and retrieve more tiles. Teams score one point for each word they create or modify in each round.

Activity reprinted by permission from Gopher Sport.

|||||||||||| Flag Frenzy ||||||||||||||||||||||||||||||||||||||||||||||||||||||||||||||||||||||||||||||||

GRADES ||||||

2–8

EQUIPMENT ||||||

- Two sets of numbered and lettered rip flags, red and yellow (these can be purchased from Gopher Sport)
- Something to write with and something to write on for each team

DESCRIPTION ||||||

A class I taught in college came up with this game, and we called it Rip Flag 100. Gopher Sport now produces this game and has renamed it Flag Frenzy. It is a strenuous activity that teaches math concepts, tagging, dodging, and teamwork. It can be played in a gym or on an athletic field divided into two equal areas (see figure 8.1).

1. Divide the class into two equal teams. Assign three generals for each team; the rest of the players are knights.

2. Each knight gets a rip flag and hangs it from his or her left hip. Give the remaining flags to the generals. The flags have numbers printed on them.

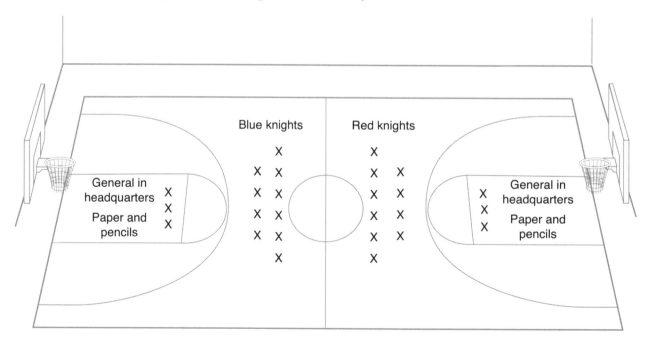

Figure 8.1 Setup for Flag Frenzy.

3. The game starts with each team of knights on their own half of the gym and their generals behind them in their intelligence headquarters, the free throw lane (see figure 8.1). Each team has something to write on and something to write with.

4. To start the game, the knights venture into the opposing team's area and attempt to capture an opponent's rip flag. When they are successful and pull off an opponent's flag, they must return it to their generals so that the generals can start adding the numbers on the captured flags. A knight cannot lose his or her flag when in possession of an opposing knight's flag and heading toward his or her generals. Knights should hold the captured flag high as they make the trip so that others know that they are off limits until they deliver the captured flag.

5. Knights who lose their flag must immediately go to their intelligence headquarters and get a new flag from their generals and reenter the game. When the generals have no more flags to hand out, the knights without flags get a desk job and become generals and help with the addition.

6. The game ends when one team has captured enough flags to total 100. The generals should yell out, "one hundred!" The opposing generals should check the addition.

7. Start another game.

VARIATIONS ||||||

- **Rip Flag Subtraction.** Each team starts with 100 points and the captured flag points are subtracted from 100.
- **Rip Flag Scrabble.** This game has several different variations, but the goal is to be the first team to spell a predetermined word. The game could be as simple as the first team to make a four-letter word wins the game. Teams could also try to make up a sentence or spell a Spanish word.

Activity reprinted by permission of Gopher Sport.

|||||||||||| Math Race |||||||||||||||||||||||||||||||||||||||||||||||||||||||||||||||||||||||||||

GRADES ||||||

1–8

EQUIPMENT ||||||

- Thirty cones or markers of some sort
- Stopwatch (optional)
- Music and player (optional)

DESCRIPTION ||||||

1. Place cones about five feet (1.5 m) apart in a straight line on a field or in the gym. Tell the students to listen carefully to your instructions because they must use their math skills as they follow along.

2. Divide the students into teams; it doesn't matter how big or small the teams are. Then ask the teams to huddle near the starting line.

3. Give each team the following written math problem on an index card. Let the teams decide if they want to figure out the answer before doing the actions or do the actions while solving the problem: Run the length of 29 cones, step backward 5 cones (24), skip forward 6 cones (30), run to the halfway point (15), gallop 5 cones forward (20), and do 10 push-ups. Subtract 11 cones and slide to that cone (9), do 20 sit-ups, now sprint forward twice that distance. Where do you end up? (18th cone)

4. When the students have figured out the answer in their teams they must do the actions in the story. Which team can get to the correct cone the quickest? Teams can go at the same time, or teams can go separately while you time them.

5. Remind students that the winner of the game is the first team with the *correct* answer. Therefore, all teams should continue solving the problem even if another team has already finished.

VARIATIONS ||||||

- Give the students several math instructions written on a piece of paper. Play music and let them run through the problems on their own.
- Add higher math functions for older students.
- Even if one team starts before other teams they may not have the correct answer.

Activity adapted, by permission, from D.R. Glover and L.A. Anderson, 2003, *Character education: 43 fitness activities for community building* (Champaign, IL: Human Kinetics), 86.

Divide and Conquer

GRADES ||||||

3–12

EQUIPMENT ||||||

- Twelve bases or poly spots with numbers 1 through 12 written or taped on top
- Stopwatch (optional)

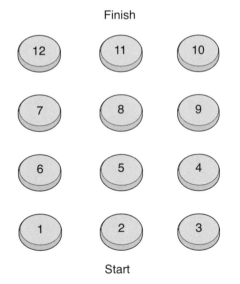

Finish

Start

Figure 8.2 Setup for Divide and Conquer.

DESCRIPTION ||||||

This challenge was created by Marc Bachman and Jay Ehlers, teachers in the team-building program offered through St. Mary's University in Winona, Minnesota. This challenge is unique because it incorporates math and puzzle skills into a team-building exercise.

The team (ideally six to eight people) must remain connected by holding hands and move through a maze of numbered bases. Each team member stands on a different base, and the sum of the numbers on the bases they are using must equal a number that can be divided by three. The group must move from one end of the maze to the other while connected, keeping the sum of the bases being used divisible by three. When the whole team has successfully moved through the maze and is standing together at the finish, the challenge is complete. Set the bases on the floor in the pattern illustrated in figure 8.2.

RULES ||||||

- Team members must stay connected during travel.
- Team members may move only one base at a time.
- Team members may move in a straight or diagonal path.
- Connected teammates must be no more than one base away from the person they are connected to.

- Only one team member may enter the maze at a time. When a teammate gets to the last row of the maze, he or she must stay connected, but may step out of the maze.
- If the sum of the bases that team members are standing on after each team member enters or exits the maze is not divisible by three, the team must start again.
- Only one person is allowed on a base at a time.
- No one should call others by their last names or use put-downs.

VARIATIONS ||||||

- To make the challenge more difficult, place the bases randomly, but make sure a number that can be divided by three is in each row.
- Time the challenge.
- Add more rows.

Adapted, by permission, from D.R. Glover and L.A. Anderson, 2003, *Character education: 43 fitness activities for community building* (Champaign, IL: Human Kinetics), 132-133. Created by Marc Bachman and Jay Ehlers.

|||||||||||| Bone Jangles ||||||||||||||||||||||||||||||||||||||||||||||||||||||||||||||||||||||||||||||

GRADES ||||||

4–8

EQUIPMENT ||||||

- One skeleton puzzle
- One deck-tennis ring
- One storage crate
- Five indoor bases
- Stopwatch
- Two gym mats

DESCRIPTION ||||||

Human anatomy and health concepts are a natural partner for physical education reinforcement. This team builder reinforces the anatomy science lessons the classroom teachers work on. This beat-the-clock challenge incorporates throwing and catching skills along with running and team communication as students attempt to put together the skeleton puzzle as quickly as they can. This game is set up for a team of eight; however, by deleting a doctor or a poly spot base it can work with fewer team members. Kids love it.

1. Place the bases about 10 to 15 feet (3-4.5 m) apart in a straight line in your gym. The distance depends on the age and ability level of your students (see figure 8.3). Place the storage crate holding the skeleton puzzle at the opposite end of the gym, or about 15 feet (4.5 m) from the fifth base. A mat is located near the first base. This serves as the medic station and the building area where the doctors assemble the puzzle.

2. Designate five students to stand on the five bases, one on each base. Station a medic and two doctors to wait on the mats near the first base. Before the challenge starts, team members should decide which five students will stand on the bases, which student will serve as the medic, and which two students will be the doctors when the game starts. This activity can be part of a team-building unit or a station with other activities going on in the gym.

3. To start the game, the student on the first base tosses the deck-tennis ring to the person on the second base. The person on base two must catch the ring and successfully turn

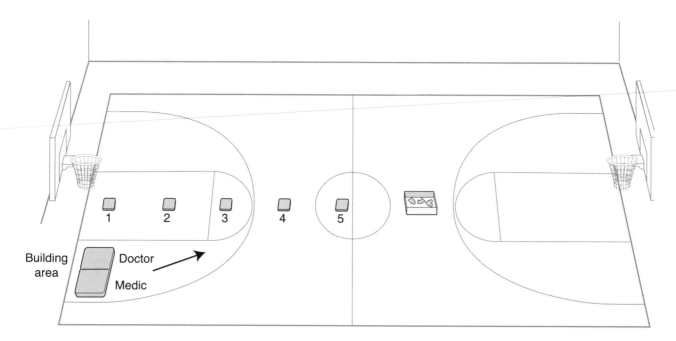

Figure 8.3 Setup for Bone Jangles.

and toss it to the person on base three. This continues until the ring has traveled to base five and then back to base one. If someone drops the ring, the players send the ring back to the person who last tossed it.

4. When the ring gets back to the first base, the medic runs to the storage crate and brings three bones back to the building area. The medic cannot leave the building area until the ring returns to base one.

5. When the medic returns, he or she gives the bones to the two doctors, who start assembling the puzzle. After the doctors receive and assemble the bones, players rotate positions. The medic moves to base one, base one moves to base two, and the other players on bases move to the next base. The student on base five becomes a doctor, and one of the doctors becomes the new medic. Players cannot rotate positions until the medic returns to the building area with three bones and the doctors assemble the bones.

6. The ring must make seven successful round trips in order for the medics to move all the puzzle pieces to the building area. After the last medic has delivered the last three puzzle pieces, teammates hustle to the building area to confer on changes that may be necessary to put Frankenstein's monster together correctly. When the team believes the puzzle is correct, the current medic yells "Bones!" This is the signal to stop the clock.

7. Check the puzzle for accuracy. If it is correct, the time stands. If it is incorrect, start the clock again while the team rearranges the bones. This process continues until Bone Jangles is correct.

VARIATIONS //////

- Allow teammates to assign permanent roles, allowing them to match players' skills with the requirements of the challenge.
- Lengthen or shorten the distance between bases.
- Bring back more or fewer bones to shorten or lengthen how long it takes to complete the challenge.

Activity adapted, by permission, from D.R. Glover and L.A. Anderson, 2003, *Character education: 43 fitness activities for community building* (Champaign, IL: Human Kinetics), 121-123.

Run for the Money

GRADES

1–8

EQUIPMENT

- One Run for the Money activity set found in the Gopher Sport catalog
- Four hurdles (optional)

DESCRIPTION

This is a currency lesson I first saw at a workshop in 2004. I wish this game had been available when I was a lot younger. Maybe I would have learned how to handle money better.

1. Place all the coins facedown inside the activity area (see figure 8.4). An activity area can be a gym or a large area, such as a soccer field. The size of the activity area depends on how much exercise you want your students to get.
2. Divide the students into four teams. Each team borders one side of the activity area.
3. When you yell "go," all teams race into the activity area at once to collect coins. Students can bring only one coin at a time back to their team's base. The running and collecting continues until all the students have collected all the coins. Each team adds up its money, and the team with the most money wins.
4. Put the coins back into the activity area and play again.

VARIATIONS

- Place a hurdle between the team and the coins. All students must go over a hurdle and over again when returning to the team before retrieving a coin.
- After retrieving a coin, students must perform five push-ups before they can take it back to their group.

Activity reprinted by permission from Gopher Sport.

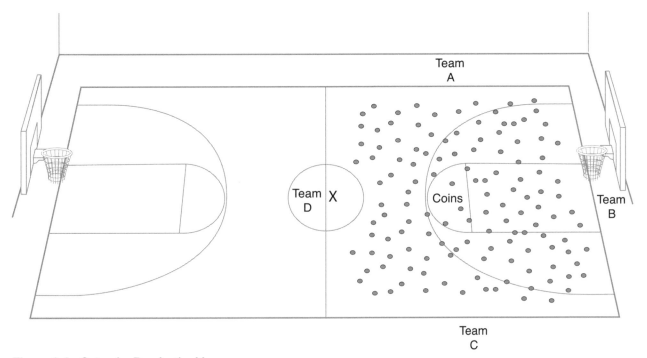

Figure 8.4 Setup for Run for the Money.

Chapter 9

Favorite Games

This chapter includes fun games that help your students practice the sport skills you taught using the activities in chapter 6 and other common sport skills like batting. Use the following suggestions to provide your students maximum opportunities for participation. Divide your class into four teams and play two separate games. Or set up even more teams with fewer players each. If the number of playing fields or courts you can set up is limited, add more equipment. For example, if you are ready to let the kids play a game of soccer and have room for only one soccer field, use two goalies per goal and two or even three foam balls, keep play continuous (when a goal is scored, the goalie simply throws the ball back into play), eliminate out-of-bounds areas, and require teams to replace goalies when a goal is scored. Use your imagination—there are many ways to involve lots of kids in these games. And remember to use equipment that is appropriate for the age of the child. For example, handing elementary-school age children an adult-size basketball will not maximize learning opportunities for your students.

Dan Midura, a physical education teacher in Roseville, Minnesota, introduced me to several games in this chapter. These games were also introduced in a book we coauthored called *The Competition–Cooperation Link,* which was published by Human Kinetics in 1999.

Popcorn Basketball

GRADES

K–6

EQUIPMENT

- One 5-foot-by-10-foot (1.5 × 3 m) 1-foot segment mat
- Thirty foam balls in assorted sizes

DESCRIPTION

This is a great basketball-shooting game. But it does not use the basketball goals.

1. Fold the mat into a circle, and set it upright on the center circle in the gym. Station two students inside the circle formed by the mat, and designate them as the popcorn basketball return machine. Using the Velcro on the ends of the mat, close the circle.

2. The rest of the students each have a ball. On your signal, they shoot the balls into the circle formed by the upright mats.

3. The two students inside throw the balls out as quickly as they can, enabling the shooting students to retrieve the balls and continue shooting. The kids inside the mats love being there, and they get a great workout.

4. After about three minutes of shooting, send two or three different students into the circle to serve as the ball returners.

5. You can let the students choose the type of shot they want to take or you can specify how they should shoot. For instance, after teaching the layup, allow the shooters to shoot only layups.

VARIATIONS ///////

- Put out two mats, one inside each free throw area. This gives more children a chance to be inside the circle.
- Forbid the students to get too close to the mats; make them shoot long shots.

Football Passing Game

GRADES ///////

3–12

EQUIPMENT ///////

- One inflatable, soft, rubber football with a textured surface that can be easily gripped or one foam football per team
- One hula hoop per two teams
- One cone per team
- Tumbling mats or crash pads if players must run close to or toward a wall or the path of another runner
- One scorecard (used by all teams)
- Two different colors of tape to mark starting lines and the location for the hula hoop

DESCRIPTION ///////

1. Divide each team evenly into passers and receivers and station each team in a different corner of the gym or playing field. In each team area, mark a starting line in one color for passers and a line in a different color for receivers. If you play this game outside, you could cut the grass shorter to mark the starting lines. Set up as many different teams as your facility allows. Figure 9.1 shows four teams playing in a gym.

2. For each team, set one football in the hula hoop near the middle of the playing space. Mark the location for the hoop with a piece of tape because the hoop will move during the course of play.

3. The passers line up in a diagonal line facing the center of the gymnasium or play area. The receivers line up on a line parallel to the end line of the basketball court, facing the cone at the other end of the court. If the cone is near a wall, stand a tumbling mat or crash pad against the wall to protect students who might run into the wall.

4. On your signal, such as a hand clap, one passer from each team runs to the team's ball, picks it up, and prepares to throw the ball to the team's receiver. The receiver may not start running until the passer touches the ball.

5. The passer attempts to throw the ball to the receiver as the receiver runs across the gym toward the cone. If the receiver catches the ball, he or she runs around the cone, back to

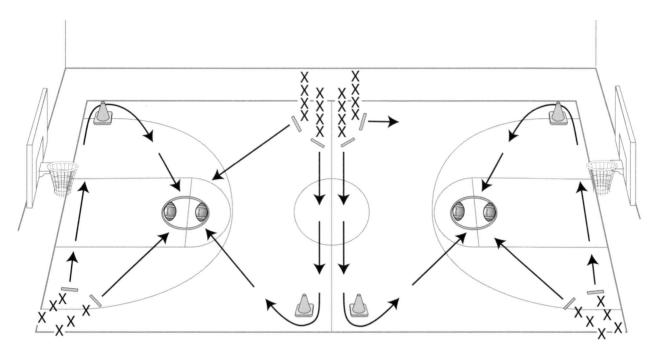

Figure 9.1   Sample setup for Football Passing Game.

the hula hoop near the center of the basketball court, and sets the ball in the hoop. If the student does not catch the ball, he or she immediately retrieves the ball and returns it to the hoop.

6. Students score points in the following manner: Receivers score one point if they catch the ball. The first receiver to catch the ball and replace it in the hoop receives a bonus point. Points can only be scored if the ball is caught. So a receiver can score two, one, or no points per turn.

7. As soon as a passer and receiver complete their turn, they return to their team, but they switch lines so that they perform the opposite task during their next turn. If a player scores, he or she runs to the scoreboard, adds his or her points, then returns to the correct line.

8. For this game to be most effective, the students must understand the movement pattern so that the game can progress rapidly. Students usually learn the pattern after going through it a few times. Once the students have learned the pattern, try to clap your hands every six to eight seconds.

Activity adapted, by permission, from D.W. Midura and D.R. Glover, 1999, *The competition-cooperation link: Games for developing respectful competitors* (Champaign, IL: Human Kinetics), 80-83.

IIIIIIIIIIIIIII **Kicking Lesson** IIIIIIIIIIIIIIIIIIIIIIIIIIIIIIIIIIIIIIIIIIIIIIIIIIIIIIIIIIIIIIIIIIIIIIIIIIIII

GRADES IIIIII

K–12

EQUIPMENT IIIIII

- One base per group of three or four
- One poly spot per group
- One ball per group (use Nerf or foam soccer balls if playing inside)
- Crash pads or tumbling mats to create a home-run fence

DESCRIPTION IIIIII

1. Place a row of bases for the kickers, one for each team, along the sideline of the basketball court. Lay out a line of poly spots for the pitchers, one for each team, down the middle of the gym at least 25 feet (8 m) from the bases (see figure 9.2).

2. If mats or crash pads are available, set up a home-run fence a reasonable distance behind the outfielders.

3. Divide the class into groups. You will need a minimum of three per group, but you might have to create bigger teams if your space limits the number of teams you can set up.

4. Give each group a numerical or alphabetical name. This description uses numbers.

5. The pitcher in group one rolls a ball to the kicker in group one. The kicker kicks the ball as far as possible, trying to get it over the home-run fence. The outfielder can try to field the ball if it does not go over the fence.

6. The kicker then jogs to the outfield and becomes the new outfielder. The pitcher jogs forward and stands behind team one's base and becomes the new kicker. The outfielder becomes the new pitcher.

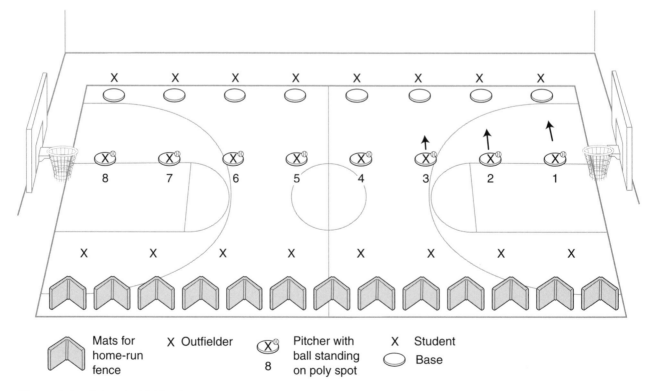

Figure 9.2   Setup for Kicking Lesson.

7. As soon as kicker one kicks the ball the pitcher in team two rolls the ball toward kicker two, who kicks the ball. The pitcher from team two jogs to base two and the outfielder from team two becomes the new pitcher.

8. The pitcher in team three rolls the ball to kicker three as soon as kicker two kicks the ball. This process continues until each team pitches a ball. As soon as the last team pitches a ball and the kicker kicks it, group one begins the process again. Theoretically, only one ball is being rolled at a time.

9. This assembly line of players continues pitching, kicking, retrieving, and so forth, until you stop them for instruction, encouragement, or other needs. You will have ample opportunity to observe all students rolling the ball and kicking it.

10. Because several students move to different places at the same time in this game, take time to teach the movement process the first time you teach this lesson.

Activity adapted, by permission, from D.W. Midura and D.R. Glover, 1999, *The competition-cooperation link: Games for developing respectful competitors* (Champaign, IL: Human Kinetics), 102-104.

IIIIIIIIIIIIII **Striking Lesson** IIIIIIIIIIIIIIIIIIIIIIIIIIIIIIIIIIIIIIIIIIIIIIIIIIIIIIIIIIIIIIIIIIIIIIIIIIIIIII

GRADES IIIIII

K–12

EQUIPMENT IIIIII

- One plastic bat per batter (If you do this lesson outdoors, you can substitute the plastic equipment for softball equipment.)
- Thirty to sixty plastic balls, such as Wiffle balls
- One base per batter
- Two cardboard boxes or other containers
- Tumbling mats

DESCRIPTION IIIIII

1. Divide your class into four groups of relatively equal size. The four groups will each begin with a different task, but eventually rotate to participate in each of the four tasks. Group one starts as the batting group. Group two begins as catchers. Group three starts as the pitcher's helpers. Group four starts as the fielders. You serve as the automatic pitching machine.

2. Set out the bases for the batters in a slightly curved line spaced far enough apart to prevent the batters from interfering with one another. Station a catcher behind each batter, far enough away that they won't be hit with a bat. The helpers stand behind you, the pitcher. Instruct them not to move in front of you while you are pitching. You will have one box of balls, and the helpers' task is to keep the other box filled with balls. As soon as you empty your box of balls, the helpers bring you a new, full box. Position the fielders at the far end of the gym. If you use the tumbling mats as a home-run fence, locate fielders on both sides of the fence.

3. Begin by throwing an underhand pitch to the first batter. Immediately after the first pitch, pitch to the second student, then to the third, and so on until you pitch to the last student in line. Then reverse the pitching order. Pitch to the last student again, and work your way back to the first (this means that the students on each end of the batting line always receive two pitches in a row after the first time through the line). Continue this process for about five minutes.

4. The batters try to hit each pitch they receive, even if it is not perfect. If a pitch is particularly bad, give that batter another pitch. If the batters miss the ball or hit a foul ball, the catchers retrieve the balls that go behind the batters and *roll* (not throw) them back to the helpers. The helpers and fielders catch and retrieve balls hit out into the gym. Fielders roll (not throw) the balls to the helpers. Fielders also try to catch as many fly balls as possible and try to rob the batters of possible home runs. The helpers continually fill the box that the pitcher is not using.

5. After about five minutes of batting, ask the students to stop and roll all balls to the helpers. Then rotate positions. The batters lay down their bats and become the new fielders. The fielders rotate forward and become the new helpers. The helpers walk forward and become the new catchers. The catchers become the new batters.

6. The automatic pitching machine begins again. Judge your time well enough that each rotation of batters gets about the same amount of time.

Adapted, by permission, from D.W. Midura and D.R. Glover, 1999, *The competition-cooperation link: Games for developing respectful competitors* (Champaign, IL: Human Kinetics), 105-108.

Zone Passing

GRADES

5–12

EQUIPMENT

- One air-filled, soft, rubber football per team (Soft inflatable rubber footballs are textured and can be caught more easily than foam balls. Older students may want to use regular footballs, but keep in mind that softer balls allow a high degree of success.)
- Scorecard
- Vinyl floor tape for marking the hiking and passing lines
- Four cones to mark point zones

DESCRIPTION

1. Divide the class into teams of three or four per team. All the teams line up at one end of the gym or playing area. The first student on each team stands at the hiking line (see figure 9.3). The second student stands on the passing line.

2. The first student hikes the ball to the passer and then runs across the gym toward the scoring zones. If the passer catches the hiked ball, the team scores one point.

3. The passer then throws the ball to the hiker, who is now the receiver. Players who catch the ball receive points based on the zone in which they make the catch: one point in zone one, two points in zone two, and three points in zone three.

4. If the receiver catches the ball, he or she keeps running toward the farthest wall, tags it, and runs the ball back to the passer. If the receiver does not catch the ball, he or she retrieves it, then runs and tags the wall and runs back to the passer.

5. While the receiver is running, the passer walks to the hiking line to become the next hiker. The receiver gives the ball to the new hiker then goes to the end of the team's line.

6. The new hiker then hikes the ball to the next student, who is the new passer, and the players repeat the process. Teammates can proceed as quickly as they can pass, run, and return the ball to the hiking line.

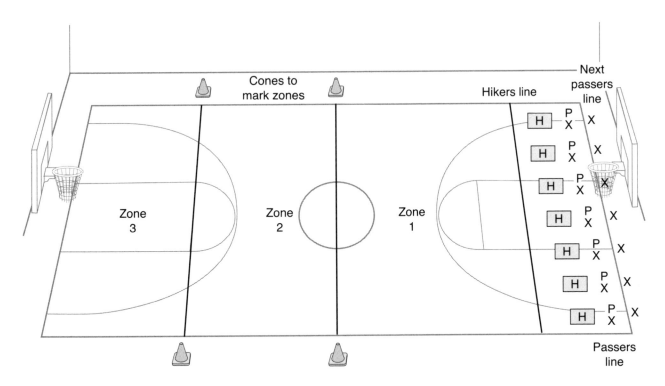

Figure 9.3 Setup for Zone Passing.

Activity and diagram adapted, by permission, from D.W. Midura and D.R. Glover, 1999, *The competition-cooperation link: Games for developing respectful competitors* (Champaign, IL: Human Kinetics), 120-123.

|||||||||||||| Power Ball ||||||||||||||||||||||||||||||||||||||||||||||||||||||||||||||||||||||||||||||

GRADES ||||||

K–12

EQUIPMENT ||||||

- Forty-five tennis balls
- Eight poly spots
- Eight softballs

DESCRIPTION ||||||

This has been one of my all-time favorite workshop activities over the last 15 years. This activity requires a lot of tennis balls. You can get them from your high school tennis coach or from a local tennis club. They have plenty of used tennis balls and will gladly donate them to you.

1. Place the poly spots in a line down one side of the gym or soccer field. Number eight sets of tennis balls one through five with a black marker. Put one softball (the power ball) with each set of five tennis balls. Place each power-ball set on a poly spot (see figure 9.4).

2. Divide the students into teams of three, and ask each team to sit down behind one of the bases. The first person in each team should roll all the balls to the other side of the gym. If you are on a soccer field, they should scatter the balls at the opposite end of the field.

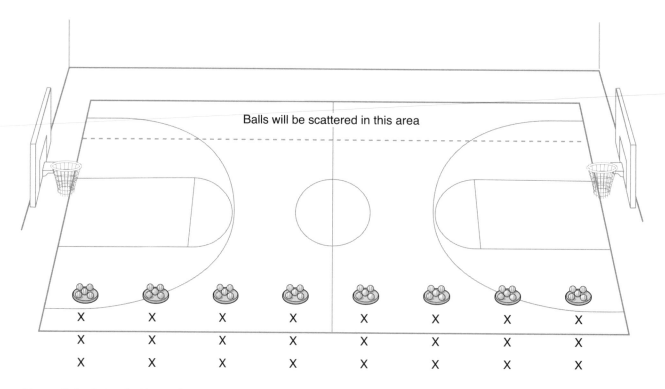

Balls will be scattered in this area

Figure 9.4   Setup for Power Ball.

3. On your signal, the first person on each team runs to the scattered balls and finds a number one ball then runs back and high-fives teammate number two, who runs out and finds a number two ball. This continues until all teams have found five numbered balls and lined them up in order on their base. The last person finds a power ball and returns it to the base.

VARIATIONS ||||||

• The first person brings back any numbered ball but must communicate which number he or she brought back so that the next runner can bring back a different number. The players must line up all the balls in order plus a power ball, but they can bring them back in any order.

• Each team brings back any six balls one at a time; it doesn't matter what number is written on them. The team adds up the numbers, and the highest score wins. Give the power ball a point value of six. Of course the teams will all be looking for the highest value ball. Give a bonus of two points to the team that finishes first. They may not have the highest point total for the six balls, but their bonus may put them in first place.

|||||||||||| Pin Basketball |||||||||||||||||||||||||||||||||||||||||||||||||||||||||||||||||||

GRADES ||||||

2–12

EQUIPMENT ||||||

• Two basketballs
• Four poly spots
• One plastic bowling pin
• One cone

DESCRIPTION ||||||

1. Divide the students into teams of 12. Half of one team lines up in one corner of the gym behind a poly spot, and the other half lines up in the opposite corner behind a poly spot. The other team lines up in the other two corners of the gym, each half behind a poly spot. Each poly spot should be the same distance from its corner (see figure 9.5).

2. Students should stand in a straight line, one behind the other, facing their teammates across the gym. Place the bowling pin in the center circle of the gym. Each team should have one basketball.

3. On your signal, a member from each team should roll the basketball toward the bowling pin, attempting to knock it over. If he or she misses, the ball will roll to the teammates lined up in the opposite gym corner. After rolling the basketball the player must rotate to the end of the line. The first teammate in line retrieves the basketball and attempts to knock down the pin. All bowling attempts must be done from the poly spot.

4. When a team knocks over the pin they earn the right to shoot layups at basket A. All 12 team members run to the free throw line at basket A and line up in single file facing the basket. This team takes turns shooting layups, counting out loud each time someone makes a shot.

5. After one team knocks over the pin, the other team immediately runs to basket B and lines up down each side of the free throw lane, passing the ball across the lane to one another and counting out the passes. When they reach 20 passes, they loudly yell "stop!" The team shooting layups must stop shooting. Both teams should sprint back to their original corners and start bowling again. While the teams are shooting and passing, the instructor replaces the pin.

6. The bowling, shooting, and passing continue until one team makes 25 layups.

7. Use two courts and four baskets for this game if possible. This will prevent students from standing around idle and allow more activity for everyone; there will only be six on a team (three in a corner).

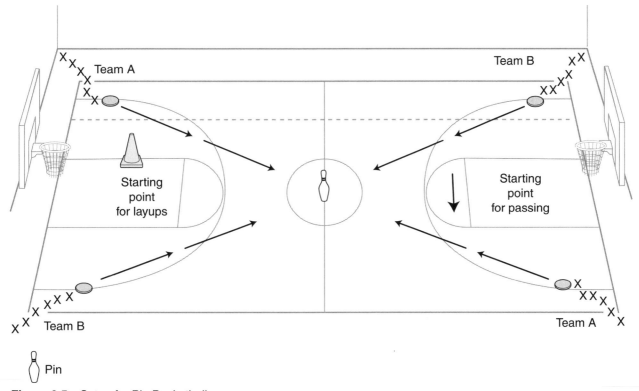

Figure 9.5 Setup for Pin Basketball.

|||||||||||||| **American Ball** ||||||||||||||||||||||||||||||||||||||||||||||||||||||||||||||||||||||||||

GRADES ||||||

3–12

EQUIPMENT ||||||

- One basketball per two teams
- Two baskets with backboards per two teams

DESCRIPTION ||||||

Students love this game. And it teaches basketball skills, such as passing, shooting, and thinking quickly on your feet.

1. Divide the students into four teams of six. Set up two courts and conduct two games simultaneously if possible. Designate two red teams and two blue teams. Line up a red and a blue team in the playing areas as shown in figure 9.6.
2. Start the game with a jump ball. The team that gains possession must try to advance the ball toward its goal—the basket it is facing—according to the following rules.

   - When a student has the ball, he or she can only advance the ball by passing. The student may not run, walk, or dribble; however, he or she may pivot as in basketball.
   - When in possession of the ball, a player has five seconds to make a pass.

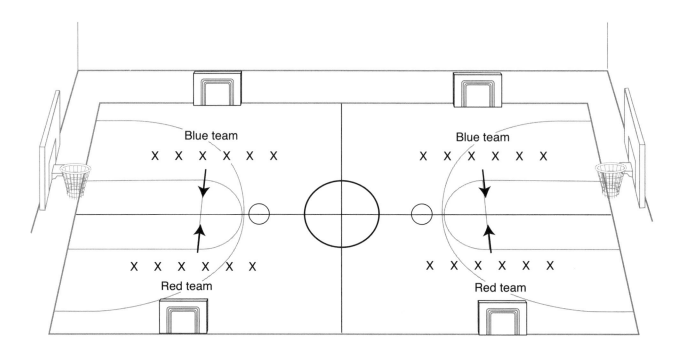

Figure 9.6   Setup for American Ball.

- Teammates who do not have the ball may move around the court to try to get in position to receive a pass from a teammate.
- If the student with the ball moves his or her feet, except to pivot, or doesn't pass the ball in five seconds, the opposing team gains possession of the ball.

3. When a team gets the ball close enough to attempt to score, the player with the ball may shoot. If the ball hits the backboard, one point is scored. If the ball hits the square behind the basket, two points are scored. If the ball goes through the basket, three points are scored. If the ball hits the square and then goes through the basket, the team still only scores three points.

4. The team on defense gains possession if they intercept a pass. They may guard the offensive team the same way basketball players defend opponents. When one team scores, the other team immediately gains possession and starts to advance the ball. It is not necessary to take the ball out of bounds as in basketball. This rule keeps the pace of the game very fast.

5. Play the game to 21 points.

6. Students can play this game with more than six on a side. You can also play it without end lines. However, if you set up four teams playing on two courts, you must establish sideline boundaries.

About the Author

Donald R. Glover has taught physical education, including adapted physical education, since 1967 at the preschool, elementary, secondary, and postsecondary levels. He currently teaches elementary physical education methods at the University of Wisconsin at River Falls.

In 1981 Glover was recognized as Minnesota's Teacher of the Year, and in 1989 he was named the Minnesota Adapted Physical Education Teacher of the Year. He has written six books, published numerous magazine and journal articles on physical education and sport, and served as a clinician at more than 100 workshops and clinics.

Glover earned his master's degree in physical education from Winona State University in 1970. A former president of MAHPERD, he is also a member of AAHPERD, NASPE, COPEC, and the Minnesota Education Association.

Don Glover is available to lead workshops and in-service sessions in physical education, character education, and team building. Please contact Don at 651-779-6904 for more information.

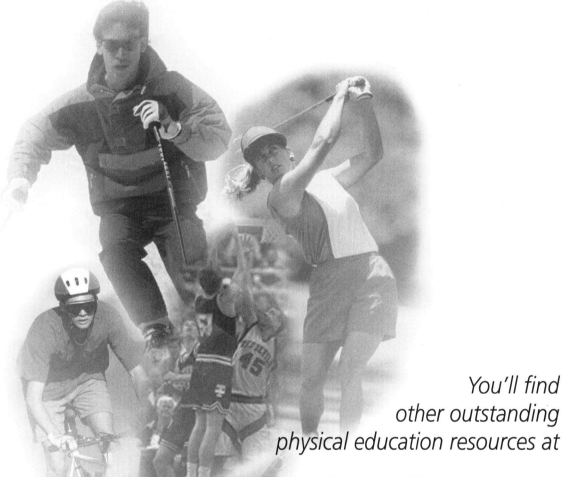